ST VINCENT
& CAMPERDOWN

By the same author

THE NATION AND THE NAVY
CAPTAIN COOK
SIR FRANCIS DRAKE
THE NAVY AND THE SLAVE TRADE
MEDICINE AND THE NAVY
THE CAPTURE OF QUEBEC
ETC.

1   *Admiral Lord Duncan*
From a mezzotint by J. R. Smith after H. P. Danloux

ST VINCENT
& CAMPERDOWN

Christopher Lloyd

LONDON
B. T. BATSFORD LTD

First published 1963

© CHRISTOPHER LLOYD, 1963

MADE AND PRINTED IN GREAT BRITAIN BY
WILLIAM CLOWES AND SONS LTD, LONDON AND BECCLES
FOR THE PUBLISHERS
B. T. BATSFORD LTD
4 FITZHARDINGE STREET, PORTMAN SQUARE, LONDON W.1

PREFACE

In *The Advancement of Learning* Bacon says that 'Just history is of three kinds, with regard to the three objects it designs to represent; which are either a portion of time, a memorable person, or an illustrious action'.

The two actions described in this book, and the memorable persons who fought them, are linked in point of time by the grand strategy adopted by the French Republic throughout the year 1797. Attempts to implement this strategy—the invasion of Ireland or England—actually began during the last days of 1796, when a blizzard defeated the attack on Bantry Bay.

It was then hoped to use the Spanish fleet in conjunction with the French ships and troops at Brest in another attempt. Although the immediate reasons for the battle of St Vincent were not directly concerned with the purposes of invasion (as Rear-Admiral Taylor has shown in his explanation of the preliminaries of the battle, proving that this was really a convoy action, though the British never realised as much), the ultimate destination of the Spanish fleet would have been Brest, had not Sir John Jervis defeated it on its way thither.

There followed the best opportunity for any scheme to invade these islands—the naval mutinies during the early part of the summer. How that unique opportunity was missed is part of our story. By the time it was planned to use the Dutch fleet for invasion purposes, now that the Spanish were out of action, the mutineers had returned to duty, and the way they fought under Duncan at Camperdown can only be explained by their determination to wipe out the stain which their behaviour during the earlier part of the year had cast upon the honour of the Royal Navy.

If ever a mass mutiny can be justified by the grievances which it seeks to redress, that at Spithead in 1797 is a notable example. Some letters which have recently come to light throw a fresh and vivid light on what happened in Duncan's fleet, and the Duncan manuscripts at the National Maritime Museum have enabled me to fill out the naval accounts of the hardest-fought action in all the long wars with France and her allies. Here again I should like to thank Rear-Admiral Taylor and the Council of the Society of Nautical Research for allowing me to reproduce the excellent plans of the battle which originally appeared in the pages of the *Mariner's Mirror* some years ago.

The battles of St Vincent and Camperdown mark the turning of the tide in the war against the French Revolution. They form the necessary prelude to the better-known victories of the Nelsonian epoch which followed, and it was on the foundation of these successes that British maritime supremacy was established to last for the next hundred years. For that reason, as well as for the biographical and narrative interest of the story, they deserve to be commemorated.

CONTENTS

THE ILLUSTRATIONS

THE ILLUSTRATIONS

English Sailor of *c.* 1795

ACKNOWLEDGMENT

The Author and Publishers wish to thank the following for permission to reproduce the illustrations appearing in this book:

The Trustees of the British Museum, for fig. 3.

The National Maritime Museum, for figs. 1, 2, 4, 8, 10–12, 17, 18, 20–2 and 24–7.

The National Portrait Gallery, for fig. 23.

The Parker Gallery, for figs. 5–7 and 9.

The Royal College of Surgeons of England, for fig. 19.

The Executors of the Duncan Family, for fig. 27.

I

Bantry Bay

ON CHRISTMAS EVE, 1796, a blizzard was blowing at Bantry Bay on the south-western tip of the Irish coast. The previous night Vice-Admiral Sir George Keith Elphinstone (later Lord Keith) brought his 74-gun ship *Monarch* into the neighbouring inlet of Crookhaven after beating against a furious snowstorm which was blowing from the north-east. This was his landfall after a three-month voyage on his return from the capture of the Cape of Good Hope. Only eight days' provisions remained on board. The Dutch prisoners on board, as well as nearly all the crew, were suffering from scurvy. The canvas was in tatters and the ship's company so enfeebled that they could not man the rigging. As Elphinstone told his sister: 'I am arrived at this *no* place after a dreadful gale of east wind for thirty-six days past. I shall sail for England the moment I can. The French are in Bantry Bay, fifteen miles off, as I am told by the natives, who request me to head them off.'

Such was the news which greeted him when he sent on shore for six chests of lemons to cure his men of scurvy. It explained the confused sound of signal guns which he heard above the whistling of the gale. But in that driving snowstorm, all was in doubt.

The customs officer at Bantry was the first to report the presence of strange sail in the broad roadstead of the bay. A hurried note to the local squire, Richard White (who was rewarded with the title of Lord Bantry after all was over) reported that: 'The French fleet consisting of twenty-eight ships of the Line and some small vessels are this moment of [*sic*] this Harbr., all beating up for Bantry what we are to do or what is to become of us God only knows.'

White immediately despatched a rider to the nearest garrison at Cork. The man rode forty-two miles in four hours through the storm and when the general received the news he had a fit and fell off his chair. 'The people under his command were sorry he recovered,' adds one of his staff.

At Cork there was also Vice-Admiral Kingsmill with one old 64-gun ship and half a dozen frigates of the Irish Guard, whose normal duty was to convoy merchantmen up-Channel when privateers were about. The idea that either he or Elphinstone should engage what sounded like the whole of the Brest fleet was ridiculous. Whether they entertained the notion or not is irrelevant: the weather made it impossible for any ship to leave her anchorage for the next week.

The expedition to Bantry Bay was the first of the many invasion plans which form the strategic thread connecting the stirring events of the year 1797. From the start of the war five years previously the French had toyed with the idea of 'planting 50,000 caps of liberty in England', but this was the first occasion on which any attempt was made to implement such a strategic pipe-dream.

The inspiration for this particular project was due to the Irish rebel (or patriot) Theobald Wolfe Tone, who called himself Adjutant-General Smith for the occasion. He had arrived from exile in the United States the previous spring and had made contact with the twenty-nine-year-old General Hoche in Paris. For years past Hoche had planned offensive action against Britain with a frivolous disregard for the difficulties involved. 'Dash and love of liberty is all that is necessary to overthrow Pitt', he told the Directory. But the British had got in first with their support of the Royalist rebels in La Vendée. Hoche made his reputation by suppressing the rebellion and now that his contemporary, the young Bonaparte in command of the Army of Italy, was reporting daily victories over the forces of reaction, Hoche was anxious to do something himself. He therefore jumped at the suggestion of the Irish patriot that a landing should be attempted in a country which was seething with unrest under the Protestant Ascendancy, and which might be expected to welcome the arrival of the French with a mass uprising on the part of fellow Catholics and Republicans. Bantry Bay offered the likeliest point of attack, a magnificent anchorage which the French had used to advantage when James II invaded the country in 1689.

But when Hoche and Tone arrived at Brest their optimism was

BRITISH BATTLES SERIES

25s   *postage 1s 9d extra*

Trafalgar *Oliver Warner*

The Capture of Quebec *Christopher Lloyd*

Waterloo *John Naylor*

Mons *John Terraine*

The Battle of the Atlantic *Donald Macintyre*

The Battle of the Nile *Oliver Warner*

The Battle of Matapan *S. W. C. Pack*

Corunna *Christopher Hibbert*

The Glorious First of June *Oliver Warner*

Battles of the English Civil War *Austin Woolrych*

Battles of the Crimean War *W. Baring Pemberton*

Coronel and the Falklands *Geoffrey Bennett*

The Battle of Arnhem *Christopher Hibbert*

Battles of the '45 *Katherine Tomasson and Francis Buist*

El Alamein *Michael Carver*

The Battle of Plassey *Michael Edwardes*

Wellington's Peninsular Victories *Michael Glover*

Please mark those books which you wish to purchase and return this
form to your bookseller

TO.. BOOKSELLER

NAME...

ADDRESS...

Value of cheque or postal order £...

B. T. BATSFORD LTD., 4 FITZHARDINGE STREET, LONDON W.1

rudely shaken. The place was in a state of chaos. The fleet was 7000 men short of complement. No volunteers could be found to man the ships which had been in harbour ever since the battle of the Glorious First of June three years earlier. Villaret de Joyeuse was still in command and he had his own hair-brained scheme of invading India; furthermore, he was a relic of the displaced Jacobin regime. Hoche has little difficulty in persuading the Directory to replace him, by Admiral Morard de Galles. But Morard had been in prison until the fall of Robespierre and he did not relish this summons to the supreme naval command. He complained that his health was bad and that he could not see a yard. 'No matter,' replied Hoche, 'we shall see for him.' Clearly, the military were in command and the navy had to carry out their plans or lose their heads. Even so, Morard told the Minister of Marine that 'the strength of the fleet is so impaired by the weakness of the ships' crews that we have everything to fear; in the event of an encounter with the enemy the expedition may be emperilled by our want of skill and precision in carrying out man-œuvres—for though I readily admit that everyone is animated with zeal and goodwill, yet these qualities unfortunately do not atone for a lack of naval force and intelligence.'

The letter shook the Directory's confidence in Hoche's plan. However their orders to postpone it arrived too late, because the armament had already sailed from Brest when their messenger reached the port. The fleet had been carried out of harbour, one might say, by the enthusiasm of Hoche and Wolfe Tone. It is not surprising that the whole affair was a muddle from the start. Taking advantage of an easterly wind, the first division of Morard's fleet put to sea on December 16. Other divisions straggled out of the road stead, one by one, until, in all, 17 ships of the line, 13 frigates and a number of small transports, making a grand total of 45 ships, with 14,750 soldiers on board, sailed from Brest.

The hinge of British naval strategy had always been the blockade of the Brest fleet. Yet this fleet sailed—and returned—without ever sighting a single British line-of-battle ship. The main portion of the Channel fleet under Lord Bridport remained, for the duration of the entire episode, safely at anchor at Spithead.

The arrangements he had made for watching the motions of the French fleet were that Vice-Admiral Sir John Colpoys with 10 or 12 of the line should cruise off Ushant and Captain Sir Edward Pellew's squadron of frigates should act as inshore scouts. This was an arrangement similar to that adopted on former occasions, even as far back as in the days of Hawke and the battle of Quiberon Bay. But, as winter came on, Pellew's squadron was reduced to one frigate, his own ship, the *Indefatigable*, and Colpoys did not make adequate arrangements about what was to happen if he was blown off his rendezvous by stress of weather. This was exactly what occurred when the French came out on December 16. Furthermore, the Admiralty as well as Bridport were to blame for allowing such a small force as that under Colpoys to attempt to contain a fleet twice its size. Colpoys' force was not the 'squadron of observation', as it was called, because Pellew was adequately fulfilling that role with his frigates, nor was it sufficient to meet the French if they should leave port. And why, if there was any chance of that happening, did Bridport continue to remain at Spithead instead of Torbay, the normal anchorage for a blockading fleet?

For a week or so Pellew was aware that something was up. He was forced to reduce his small force by sending his smaller ships to warn the Admiral with the intelligence that between 26 and 29 ships of the line were evidently preparing to put to sea. For his part, the French admiral was well aware of what Pellew was doing, so the day before the fleet sailed the *Indefatigable* was herself chased off station.

When the French sailed they steered a southerly course before turning west, in order to avoid any possible clash with Colpoys off Ushant. For the first day Pellew shadowed them; but, since his was the only British frigate in contact, all he could do was to add to their obvious confusion by firing meaningless signal guns during the hours of darkness. After that he decided to rejoin Colpoys in the firm belief that his warnings had been received and that the admiral had prepared some counter-measures.

But the admiral was nowhere to be found, and when some of the detached frigates rejoined Pellew they had to report that his warnings had never been delivered. All he could now do was to send a fast lugger with a despatch direct to the Admiralty and himself withdraw northward to Falmouth as the gale increased. 'God knows, my lord,' he told the First Lord of the Admiralty, 'if I shall be doing is right, but left in a wilderness of conjecture I can only say that the sacrifice of my life would be easy, if it served my gracious King and my country.'

Colpoys, in fact, had made no attempt to ride out the storm. He had fallen back, not on Torbay, but as far east as Spithead. When all was over and it was known that the French fleet had been missed, this course of action did his reputation no good. A few months later the mutineers at Spithead were singing a ballad in which it was complained that

> *When the enemy of Britain was ploughing the sea,*
> *He, like a base coward, let them get away,*
> *When the French and their transports sailed to Bantry Bay.*

Meanwhile the enemy fleet had continued, not as Pellew imagined, to the southward but to the west in order to steer for Mizen Head at the entrance of Bantry Bay. This cape was sighted on December 22 after a stormy passage in the depth of winter—the worst gale, said Pellew, that he had ever experienced at sea. All but seven vessels made the shelter of the roadstead, but one of these was the frigate carrying the admiral and the general. For some reason Morard and Hoche had elected to sail in a frigate rather than a ship of the line, as was customary. They soon became separated from the main body of the fleet and they never resumed contact until all was over. It is true that Morard once sighted some lights ahead of him, but he imagined them to be those of British ships and therefore altered course further to the westward. In consequence he only arrived at Bantry Bay after all his other ships had left.

However sheltered the bay, the ships had a very uncomfortable few days there. The north-east wind which had carried them out of Brest steadily freshened, until it turned into a blizzard. Snow was falling before they even sighted land. Wolfe Tone was on board the ship carrying Vice-Admiral Nielly and General Grouchy, better known for his famous mistake at Waterloo eighteen years later. All arrangements for the disposition of the ships and for landing by boats had been made with meticulous care by Bruix, now a commodore but later Napoleon's most successful admiral until his death in the year of Trafalgar. It seems that he was indeed responsible for the choice of Bantry as the point of disembarkation.

A better choice for a landing place could not have been made.

The bay, much used in the nineteenth century for manœuvres and for regattas, is an eighteen-mile-long stretch of water four miles broad and well sheltered from the prevalent south-westerly winds. Since the little town of Bantry was forty-two miles from the nearest garrison at Cork and was only held by 400 yeomanry under the command of the local squire, disembarkation could be carried out without interference. The Government had not even provided these men with uniforms, so that they were liable to be shot out of hand, and Irish roads being what they were it was unlikely that any regular troops could arrive for some days after the alarm was given.

Irish agents had assured the Directory that the peasantry would welcome the invaders with enthusiasm. There was no sign of this when they arrived on that bleak December day, indeed there was hardly any sign of land at all, because of the blizzard blowing from the east. It was tantalising for a patriot like Tone to be within a stone's throw of his native land and yet be unable to reach it. The weather had already damped the optimism of his fellow officers. 'I was burning with rage', he writes in his diary on the day of arrival, 'however, I said nothing, and will say nothing until I get ashore, if ever I am so happy as to arrive there. We are gaining the Bay by degrees, with a head wind at east, where it has hung these five weeks. Tomorrow we hope, if nothing extraordinary happens, to cast anchor in the mouth of the Bay and work up tomorrow morning: these delays are dreadful to my impatience. I am now so near the shore that I can distinctly see two old castles, yet I am utterly uncertain whether I shall ever set foot on it.'

More ships came in during the next few days and spirits began to rise, somewhat irresponsibly, if we are to believe Tone: 'It is an enterprise truly unique: we have not a guinea; we have not tent; we have not a horse to draw our four pieces of artillery; the General in chief marches on foot; we leave all our baggage behind us; we have nothing but the arms in our hands, the clothes on our backs, and a good courage, but that is sufficient. With all these original circumstances, such as I believe were never found united in an expedition of such magnitude as that we are about to attempt, we are all as gay as larks. . . . We purpose to make a race for Cork, as if the devil were in our bodies, and when we are fairly there, we will stop for a day or two to take breath and look about us.'

In the absence of General Hoche, Grouchy proposed to land the first 6000 men on Christmas Day, but another snowstorm on Christmas Eve prevented this, so that Tone began to be 'devoured by the gloomiest reflections' once more. Ships were beginning to drag their anchors. Troops were either sickening from being cooped up so long under hatches, or were shivering from wet and cold on the upper decks. Already some of the more faint-hearted captains were beating out of the bay without orders and there were cries on board many ships of '*Coupez vos cables—appareillez.*'

After less than a week in the bay, during which time not a man was landed nor a shot fired and all that could be heard was the howling of the gale, Nielly decided to return to Brest as the wind began to come round to south-west. Even Tone had given up hope: 'There only wants our falling in with the English to complete our destruction; and, to judge the future by the past, there is every probability that that will not be wanting. All our hopes are now reduced to get back in safety to Brest and I believe that we will set sail for that port the instant the weather will permit. I confess, myself, that I now look upon the expedition as impracticable. . . . This infernal wind continues without intermission, and now that all is lost I am as eager to get back to France as I was to come to Ireland.'

By New Year's Day there was not a ship left on the Irish coast. The concluding entry in Tone's diary reads: 'I am utterly astonished that we did not see a single English ship of war, neither going nor coming back.' There were two exceptions to this. A frigate was driven on shore near Cork, where Kingsmill took the crew prisoners and for the first time discovered the magnitude of the danger. Bridport was promptly informed, but the Channel fleet only reached Bantry Bay on January 9, over a week after the French had left. And just as Pellew had been the only officer to see the enemy leaving Brest, so his frigate, now accompanied by the 36-gun *Amazon*, was the only ship back on station to witness their return.

On January 13, some fifty leagues south-west of Ushant, he sighted a large French ship of the line which had apparently parted company with the main body. She was the *Droits des Hommes*, 74. Her captain recognised the *Indefatigable* because she was a familiar sight on the approaches to Brest harbour. He did not intend to surrender to a couple of mere frigates, even after the gale had carried away his fore and main topmasts. Seeing that she was 'steering very wild', Pellew determined to close, though the *Amazon* was then seven miles astern. His first attempt to run her on board failed because the big ship's bowsprit passed over the frigate's quarter-deck. By the time he had brought his ship round again, the *Amazon* had come up, but at such a spanking pace that she shot ahead of the enemy before she could bring to. The presence of 7000 soldiers crowding her lower decks prevented the French ship from using her heavier armament, but volleys of musketry continued through the hours of darkness.

The two frigates, writes Pellew in his despatch, then 'commenced a second attack, placing ourselves, after some raking broadsides, upon each quarter and this attack, often within pistol shot, was by both ships unremitted for above five hours, when we sheered off to secure our masts'.

This was at two o'clock in the morning. An hour later drums beat to quarters for a third attack. By this time the three ships had drifted near the rocky coast of the mainland, though no one realised the danger in the darkness: 'the sea was high, the people on the main-deck were up to their middles in water, some guns broke their breechings four times, and some drew the ring bolts from the sides. All our masts were much wounded, the main topmast completely unrigged and saved only by uncommon alacrity.'

Pellew's pilot was a Breton Royalist. When the captain imagined that he was in the bay leading to Brest, he gave orders to cease fire and haul to the northward. The pilot shouted, 'Non, non, mon capitaine—de oder way.' As he altered course to the southward he hoisted signal lanterns to warn the *Amazon* to do the same, but there were no answering signals. Soon after, Pellew found himself danger-ously embayed in Audierne Bay, with wicked rocks looming up ahead of him as the day dawned.

First light revealed the *Droits des Hommes* a total wreck on a sand-bank a mile away. It was essential for the *Indefatigable* to bear up for Falmouth before anything could be done about her. From there he wrote to the First Lord:

> I fear your lordship will think me rather imprudent on this occasion, but what can be done if an enemy's coast is always to frighten us and give them protection as safely as their ports? If Lord Hawke had no

2 *Thomas Ramsay, Nelson's boatswain*
From a watercolour drawing by
P. J. de Loutherbourg

3 *The Earl of St. Vincent in old age*
From a drawing by M. K. Jervis, 1816

4   *Nelson receiving the surrender of the captain of the 'San Josef'*
From a painting by Daniel Orme

fears for a lee shore with a large fleet under his charge, could I for a
moment think of two inconsiderable frigates? I was anxious to tow this
nondescript to England; for indeed, my lord, I cannot tell you what
she was. All those about me believe her a ship of the line without a
poop. . . . I have great doubt any person can be saved; the surf was
tremendous and beating quite over them. I have placed him on the
chart about three or four miles to the southward of Audierne town.
She must have suffered prodigiously; our expenses alone was above
100 barrels of powder. I never experienced such fatigue. The ship was
full of water, the cockpit half-leg deep, and the surgeon absolutely
obliged to tie himself and patient to the stanchions to perform an
amputation.

Soon afterwards came the news that the *Amazon* had also run
aground near the *Droits des Hommes*. Captain Reynolds and all his
crew were taken prisoner, but their ship was a total loss.

Apart from the loss of this line-of-battle ship, some ten vessels,
mostly transports, of the French armada failed to return to port.
Such losses were due entirely to the weather: the British fleet had
little to congratulate itself upon in the story of the Bantry Bay expedition. Indeed, neither side emerged with much credit. The French
plan was inept from the start—the wrong time of year, an ill-
equipped and worse-led fleet, which was completely untrained. But
had they landed in Ireland they would have found little to oppose
them and might indeed have roused the natives to take up arms, as
in the days of James II.

As for the British, they had ample warning in the King's speech
three months previously that there was 'a design of invading these
kingdoms'. The principal blame for the faulty disposition of the fleet
must lie on the shoulders of the sluggish Lord Bridport and ultimately those of Spencer, the First Lord. The weather gave Colpoys
some excuse, but the fact remains that he did not cruise upon his
rendezvous. Only Pellew did his duty, apart from those like Kingsmill
and Elphinstone who found themselves unwittingly involved because
of their presence on the Irish coast.

The failure of the Channel fleet had its repercussions a few months
later, because it is no coincidence that the great mutinies broke out
in that fleet, with its ignoble record, and not in the Mediterranean
fleet, which Jervis was to lead to victory only a month after this

fiasco. Had succeeding events been of the same pattern as Bantry Bay, the year 1797 would not have been worth writing about, since it would have passed into as deep an obscurity as the preceding years of the war. Instead, the attempted invasion of Ireland was the curtain-raiser of the most glorious years of the war at sea.

2

The Mediterranean Fleet

AT THE ENTRANCE of the Painted Hall at Greenwich there used to stand two statues, those of Lord St. Vincent and Lord Nelson, the master and the pupil. At the date of the battle of St. Vincent, from which Sir John Jervis took his title, the commander-in-chief of the Mediterranean fleet was sixty-two years of age, yet when he hoisted his flag in the *Victory* he expressed his diffidence at being so young to command so large a squadron. In that year Commodore Horatio Nelson was thirty-eight and General Napoleon Bonaparte only twenty-seven. Had all three men died when Jervis was appointed to the command, none of them would ever have been heard of again.

Moreover, had not Jervis previously commanded in the Mediterranean and later in the Channel, Nelson would never have received the ships and men which he led to victory in the succeeding eight years. He spoke no more than the truth when he wrote after the battle of the Nile to the old man who first discerned his genius: 'We look to you, as we have always found you, as to our Father, under whose fostering care we have been led to fame.'

'Fostering care' was a phrase which was variously interpreted, according to which side of the fence people found themselves in their relationship with this formidable disciplinarian. The wives of officers in the Channel fleet, when they heard of St. Vincent's appointment to that command, raised their glasses to the toast: 'May the discipline of the Mediterranean fleet never be introduced to the Channel.' The physician of the fleet, when he was sent home from the Mediterranenan, complained that he had been dismissed 'by the tyranny and duplicity of Lord St. Vincent.' On the other hand, Collingwood, and indeed all who served under him in a crisis, asked:

'Should we not be grateful to him who had such confidence in his fleet that he thought no force too great for him?'

As a leader of men St. Vincent might have taken for his motto the words of Frederick the Great: 'Men must be made to fear their officers more than danger; the slightest loosening of discipline will lead to barbarisation.' Nelson gained the confidence of his men by love for them and a consideration of their needs. St. Vincent led them by the fear of the lash and by the force of his example. He possessed just that strength of personality which commanded respect and loyalty at a time when the bonds of discipline were cracking because of the indolence, the 'gimcrack and frippery', which he discerned in so many officers before the outbreak of the naval mutinies. There was no mutiny in the fleet which he commanded, and many of the customs which he introduced to tighten up the behaviour of officers and men have lasted until today—the ceremony of the Colours in the morning and the evening, for example, or the custom of uncovering when the National Anthem is played. Curiously enough, he regarded the habit of adding the letters R.N. to an officer's name as 'flippant and pert, and means nothing'.

John Jervis differed from most of the officers he was to command in that he possessed no 'interest' to further his career in the service. The son of a civil servant who held the post of treasurer of Greenwich Hospital, he ran away to sea as a boy. When brought home again, his father told him that he could join the Navy if he understood that beyond £20 in his pocket and a suit of clothes, nothing further could be provided for him. Recalling in his old age how his first coat hung down to his heels because he bought it second-hand, and how he was compelled to make a pair of trousers out of his bed linen, he told his biographer 'with great energy': 'From that time to this I have taken care to keep within my means.' Since he was thus compelled to live on his pay, and since he earned his advancement entirely by his own efforts, he consistently frowned on the irresponsible exercise of patronage. He was a man totally dedicated to the service, so that when in his turn he came to wield very considerable powers of patronage as a commander-in-chief or as First Lord of the Admiralty, he never promoted those who were merely exploiting friendship or interest in influential circles.

His naval career is one of the longest on record, just as Nelson's is one of the shortest. Jervis entered the Navy at the age of thirteen in 1747. He resigned his last command in 1807 at the age of seventy-three, though he did not die until 1823. Up to the time of the battle of St. Vincent, when he was sixty-two, he was unknown outside the service. Three years later he was First Lord, being one of the last serving officers to hold that post.

His first independent command was in 1759, when he was appointed to the *Porcupine* sloop to assist Wolfe's first attempt to dislodge Montcalm's troops at Quebec. Wolfe had been to the same school at Greenwich and was a close personal friend of Jervis, but the story that the night before the final attack on the Heights of Abraham he entrusted to his hands a miniature to give to his fiancée cannot be substantiated, because at the moment the *Porcupine* was several miles down-river.

It was an astonishing length of time which the old man could look back on when he retired to his house near Torquay: from the capture of Quebec to the surrender of Napoleon. His devotion to the service had been untiring. His judgement on naval affairs was valued because of its integrity and frankness. In politics his prejudices were more apparent: he called himself a royalist Whig, which meant, in effect, a keen dislike of William Pitt and a fanatical devotion to George III, who referred to him as 'my old oak'.

In religious matters—and he was a deeply religious man—he defended the Established Church with his customary acerbity against all Dissenters. Every one of his private letters is stamped with his strong personality, which makes them so eminently quotable, but none is more characteristic than the following to the Secretary of the Admiralty on the subject of the future Lord Barham, a noted Methodist, who was First Lord in the year of Trafalgar:

My dear Nepean,—That damned fellow Sir Charles Middleton, after making more money by the sale of offices at the Navy Board than any of his predecessors, comes to the Admiralty with his cant, imposture, hoards of precedents and scraps of tape and buckram, and makes you all believe that he is the only man capable of regulating your proceedings, when he is really and truly fit for nothing but new-modelling your correspondence with Port Admirals etc., for he neither possesses a mind to direct great features, nor was ever in a situation as an officer to acquire knowledge or experience: the utmost extent of his abilities having gone no further than the forming and swaddling system of morality for his ship's company and compiling with the aid of that dull dog Patton the most voluminous stupid code of signals that has been exhibited by the signalmongers of the present age.

He once said that 1782 was 'a memorable year for me. I committed three great faults—I got knighted, I got married and I got into parliament.' The first was due to a remarkable single-ship action in which he captured a French 74-gun ship without the loss of a man. The second was a violation of one of his own rules, that married officers were not worth their salt. According to him, if an officer married young he was lost to the service and might receive, as did one unlucky fellow, the following sort of missive:

'Sir, You, having thought fit to take to yourself a wife, are to look for no further attentions from your humble servant, Jervis.'

Unfortunately, the letter misfired. It reached a Lieutenant Bayntum, who was not even contemplating matrimony and replied to the admiral 'in all astonishment' that he 'abhorred matrimony' as much as he did. It turned out that Lady Jervis had sent the reproof to the wrong man, who for his part had received the favourable letter which the admiral had intended for Bayntum.

His zeal for the service naturally made his own ship, the *Foudroyant*, the crack ship in the fleet before the war. When he was promoted rear-admiral at the commencement of hostilities he was appointed to the naval command of a combined operation in the West Indies. It was not the enemy but yellow fever which ruined the expedition, from which Jervis was invalided home after narrowly escaping with his life.

What is surprising, in view of his opposition to Pitt's direction of the war, is that he was appointed to the highly responsible post of commander-in-chief of the Mediterranean fleet in the summer of 1795. This was done at the instance of the new First Lord, Lord Spencer, when the vacancy arose on account of the illness of the admiral out there. The suggestion was apparently made in the first place by Admiral Duncan, who succeeded Jervis in command of the *Foudroyant* and whose career occupies the second part of this book.

Jedediah Tucker, his secretary and biographer, gives the following account of Jervis's daily routine in that post:

His hours of rising in the morning, and retiring at night, were generally very early. His table was always handsomely appointed, and liberally surrounded; his manners at it, those of a high-bred gentleman. Of the conversation, politics formed no part; though his sentiments on them were decided and strong, yet knowledge of his party could not be acquired, still less felt, from him by any one under his command. Political bias affected not the promotion he bestowed. A meritorious officer, or, likelier still, the meritorious son of an old officer, especially if without interest, was generally promoted before those backed by the influence of the powerful. The stern performance of duty, whether it were of importance, or the most transient trifle, he carried on with punctilious ceremony, and with a gravity of demeanour amounting almost to solemnity; but when disengaged from it, he would sometimes beam forth in gaiety and playfulness, of which also his sailor-mind was constituted.

This more affable aspect of the formidable old admiral is well illustrated in the diary of Betsy Wynne, the wife of Captain Fremantle. She met him for the first time soon after he came out to the Mediterranean. 'We dressed to go to the *Victory*. The admiral was on deck to receive us with the greatest civility and kindness; nothing stiff or formal about him, and we were not at all embarrassed, as I feared we should be. He desired that we should pay the tribute which was due to him on entering his cabin. This was to kiss him, which the ladies did very willingly. . . . The old gentleman is very partial to kisses.'

2

War in the Mediterranean had opened two years previously with a most satisfactory event: the defection of the French fleet and the occupation of Royalist Toulon by forces under the command of Lord Hood. But as soon as a Revolutionary battery had been sited on a hill overlooking the harbour by an unknown artillery officer of Corsican origin, the place became untenable. Hood took some 18 French warships out of the port with him, but he failed to destroy the 27 which he left behind. From that date the British position in the Mediterranean steadily deteriorated.

The intended governor of Toulon, Sir Gilbert Elliot, later Lord Minto, was sent to rule the newly acquired island of Corsica instead. It was here, at the siege of Calvi, that Nelson lost the sight of his eye:

he made little of the injury at the time, but six months later he could scarcely use his right eye. When Hood returned home, he was succeeded by Sir William Hotham and something like apathy descended on the fleet. Hotham was a lethargic character, who gave the able young captains under his command little chance to show the quality of their mettle. True, Captain Nelson of the *Agamemnon* (64 guns) did take the French 74, *Ça Ira*, in a brilliant action shortly before Jervis's arrival, but except for the capture of Corsica there was no opportunity for British arms to shine. Nor could the new commander-in-chief, when he arrived in the summer of 1795, do more than wait on events and make sure that Toulon was closely blockaded.

It was the French army who made the first moves when the Revolution moved into its expansionist phase on the Rhine and in northern Italy. In the spring of 1796 Bonaparte was appointed to the command of the Army of Italy, a body of ragamuffins with orders to clear the old professional army of Austria out of Italy. The First Italian Campaign made the reputation of the young general by marking the beginning of a series of collapses on the part of Britain's Continental allies. As he watched with unwilling admiration the advance of the French, which he could hinder but not check, Nelson told his wife: 'England will soon carry on the war alone, if she is still determined to go on, and instead of having all Europe in our alliance and pay, we shall have them in a certain degree all against us.' A few days later—June 13, 1796—he accurately prophesied the future character of the war: 'Indeed, the French say we are masters on shore and the English at sea.'

Apart from its contemporary success in giving France the control of the whole peninsula when the Venetian Republic disappeared after so many centuries of existence and even Tuscany and Naples made their peace, Bonaparte's campaign introduced a new and sinister concept of warfare: that of totalitarian war with a conscript army living off the country, flouting all the accepted rules of war and winning the sort of decisive victories which eighteenth century generals never contemplated. Such victories, however, inevitably led to further wars of nationalist revolt and revenge.

In 1795 France had over-run the Low Countries and set up the Batavian Republic in Holland. In 1796 this was followed by the

Cisalpine Republic in Italy and in August that year Spain concluded an ignoble alliance with Revolutionary France which led to a declaration of war with Britain in October. With the coasts around the Gulf of Lions, and above all the port of Leghorn closed to him, Jervis's position in the Mediterranean became untenable. Hoping against hope that the Austrian alliance might be revived, the British government delayed evacuating the remaining bases in Corsica and Elba, but neither were satisfactory for replenishing a fleet. According to Captain Collingwood, Corsica produced nothing but wild hogs, assassins and generals of the calibre of Bonaparte. Thus it was shortage of supplies, not the 17 line-of-battle ships in Toulon harbour, nor the even greater number of Spanish ships at Cadiz and Cartagena, which forced Jervis's fleet (never numbering more that 13 of the line) out of the Mediterranean. He did not have to wait until the treaty of Campo Formio in May 1797 set the seal on the French conquests of the previous year. With singular prescience he wrote: 'The French certainly do pursue their objects with perseverance, and all the powers of Europe, except Russia, will soon be instruments in their hands against us.' The army which Napoleon was to lead up to the gates of Moscow had begun its march.

3

The most remarkable example of training a fleet under wartime conditions and in the face of adverse news from every quarter was that achieved by Sir John Jervis during the eighteen months which preceded the battle of St. Vincent, that is to say between the date when he hoisted his flag in the *Victory* in June 1795 and the date when he evacuated the Mediterranean in December 1796.

When he took over from Hotham, he found the fleet 2000 men under strength. Its morale was low and its health worse. For twelve months he bombarded the First Lord with complaints about shortages of planks, nails, lead, twine, oars, masts, yards and canvas. The few frigates which he had at his disposal were almost unserviceable, and the ships of the line sent out to reinforce him were a disgrace to the dockyards at home. The *Goliath*, for instance, had only recently been refitted, but Jervis found her almost unseaworthy.

In general, as he told the Navy Board in one of his many angry letters to the Commissioners, 'the ships are a complete sieve from the poop to the orlop deck, both in the decks and the sides'. Nor did his methods of close blockade, which meant being at sea sometimes for twenty-four weeks at a stretch, spare the weather-beaten ships cruising in the Gulf of Lions.

As to health, there were at that date four principal diseases to combat at sea: scurvy, typhus, malaria and venereal disease. The year in which he took up his command is a landmark in the history of scurvy, that most ancient curse of the sea, because it was then that Sir Gilbert Blane, head of a newly constituted Sick and Hurt Board, persuaded the Admiralty to make a regular issue of lemon juice—forty years after Dr. James Lind had proved by the first controlled dietetic experiment in history the efficacy of this preventive (lime juice, which later replaced it, is less than half so valuable). Dr. Harness, physician of Jervis's fleet, introduced it into the Mediterranean fleet, though the admiral sensibly preferred fresh lemons and onions when he could get them. He never had a high opinion of medical officers, and though he began by referring to Harness as 'a skilful physician and a diligent and conscientious man', he soon quarrelled with him and replaced him by the one doctor for whom, apart from Blane, he had any regard—Dr. John Weir.

Typhus (ship or gaol fever, as it was then called) is a disease associated with colder climates, since it is a louse-borne disease common to those who keep their clothes on too long: more soldiers have died, particularly in eastern Europe, from epidemics of typhus than have ever been killed by shot or shell. Another of Blane's innovations was responsible for its low incidence in Jervis's fleet— the introduction of soap in 1796. So little had the authorities cared about the health of seamen during the previous decades that far more attention was paid to keeping clean the decks of a ship than the bodies of those who trod them. But even if soap was now available, its use was restricted by the difficulties of supplying the ships with water. The admiral threatened to send home all sailors 'wives' who had come out as washerwomen or nurses and whom he suspected of wasting the precious fresh water supply, if they did not mend their ways.

Malaria, whose very name betrays its Italian origin, was a much more serious menace: at one time there were 150 cases on board the *Agamemnon*, of whom Nelson was one. Things would have been much worse had more time been spent on shore, but in that case venereal disease would have become even more rampant. Men went on shore at Leghorn and picked it up there, or prostitutes ('those vermin' as Jervis called them) came on board the ships as they lay at anchor. One of his first disciplinary actions was to send them all on shore.

Among the stream of orders issued to the ships under his command was one demanding a weekly report that all bedding had been aired. Another laid down that clothes should be washed once a week. A third instructed all surgeons to carry their instruments with them at all times. By such methods, Nelson claimed, 'You taught us to keep seamen healthy without going into port, and to stay at sea for years without a refit.'

More obvious methods of working up the fleet into a high state of efficiency were the regular gunnery drills and tactical exercises. Soon every captain knew exactly what to do when the flagship altered course. Since in the days of warfare under sail a close-hauled line of battle was essential, and since every sailing ship had her own peculiarities and every admiral his own method of signalling, Jervis reminded his captains that a good look-out must be kept night and day for whatever signal was shown on board the *Victory* and that they themselves were responsible for keeping station and not only the master of the ship, 'having observed with equal surprise and concern that some of the fast-sailing ships have frequently failed from this omission, while the worst going have stayed. A sharp look-out should be continually kept by the ships astern, and they held in readiness to throw all aback, or keep the wind close, to keep clear of a ship ahead missing.'

By such methods, he reminded the First Lord, this fleet was not to be regarded as other fleets: 'We have no relaxation in port, where we never go without positive necessity; the officers are all kept to their duty; no sleeping on shore, or rambling about the country; and when at sea we do not make snug for the night, as in the Western Squadron (the Channel Fleet), but are working incessantly by the lead to keep our position, insomuch as both mind and body are continually upon the stretch.'

37

The chief trouble when he arrived was the defeatist state of mind of the officers. Hotham might have gone, but Vice-Admiral Man remained. 'Poor Admiral Man', he told Spencer when there was talk of replacement, 'has been afflicted with such a disturbed mind during the last nine months that imaginary ills and difficulties have been continually breeding in it. When the Blue Devils prevail, there is an end of resource and energy. . . . I beg I may have no more admirals, unless they are firm men.'

'Fortunately for me', he continues in another letter, 'Commodore Nelson and several of the captains on the line-of-battle ships and frigates under my command are of a temper that will work to anything.' It was to this group of natural leaders, Nelson's future Band of Brothers, that he found he could address himself. For those who were slower to follow his lead, this is the sort of fleet order which he was in the habit of issuing:

> To the Respective Captains.—The Admiral having observed a flippancy in the behaviour of officers when coming upon the *Victory*'s quarterdeck, and sometimes in receiving orders from a superior officer, and that they do not pull off their hats, and some not even touch them: it is his positive direction, that any officer who shall in future so far forget this essential duty of respect and subordination, be publicly admonished.   J. JERVIS.

4

Before the battle is joined, in which nearly all his captains distinguished themselves and the fruits of eighteen months of such training became apparent, the opportunity may be taken of considering the sort of officers Jervis had with him. Today their names form a beadroll of honour unparalleled at any other period, but when he first commanded them they were unknown. All of them had earned promotion during the War of American Independence. Many had fought with Howe at the Glorious First of June in 1794 before being posted to the Mediterranean. Others had been stationed there since the outbreak of war.

Of these Captain Horatio Nelson of the *Agamemnon* was of course pre-eminent, though his ship was the least fit for service on account of the length of time she had spent at sea. When Jervis arrived Nelson told his wife that 'Sir John was a perfect stranger to me, therefore I feel the more flattered'—at the attention he received and the quick understanding that grew up between them. As a matter of fact they had met once before, long before the war, when Jervis was a Member of Parliament. Nelson was walking down a passage in the Treasury building with his patron, Captain Locker, when they happened to meet Jervis. As an old friend, Locker took the opportunity to introduce his *élève*. Such a chance meeting probably made little impression on a man who was forty years Nelson's senior, but he had not been in the Mediterranean long before he began to sing Nelson's praises in his letters home. These are so full of references to Nelson's zeal and activity on all occasions that he was soon promoted from captain to commodore. 'In short,' Jervis told him, 'there is nothing within my grasp that I shall not be proud to confer on you.' The old *Agamemnon* was sent home and Nelson told to transfer his broad red commodore's pendant to a bigger and better ship, the *Captain* of 74 guns.

When Nelson came out to the Mediterranean he brought with him his fourteen-year-old stepson, Josiah Nisbet, and William Hoste, the son of a neighbouring clergyman. As midshipmen, they were happy and efficient young men. It was not till later that Josiah's faults became apparent and Nelson had too much integrity to overlook them, though he did his best for the boy. Hoste, on the other hand, lived to become one of the most distinguished frigate captains of the age.

In command of the *Captain* (since Nelson was a commodore) was Captain Ralph Willett Miller, of whom Nelson said that he was 'the only truly virtuous man I ever knew'. Born at New York in 1762, he entered the Royal Navy in order to fight the rebels, his father being a leading loyalist. Miller went out to the Mediterranean with Lord Hood at the beginning of the war, but the *Captain* was his first command. For the next year or two he and Nelson were inseparable. He was Nelson's right-hand man at the battle of St. Vincent. He fought with him in the boat attack at Santa Cruz, where Nelson lost his arm. He fought at the Nile as captain of the *Theseus*. The Navy never lost a better officer when he was killed at the siege of Acre the next year, for Miller was one who is described by his contem-

poraries as combining the intrepidity of a Nelson with the determination of a Troubridge.

Thomas Troubridge, now captain of the *Culloden*, had been Nelson's
friend for the past twenty-five years, from the days when they were
midshipmen together in the West Indies. The son of a baker of
Irish descent, he always spoke with a marked brogue. For Nelson he
had an almost feminine affection, and he more than any other was
shocked by the affair with Emma Hamilton which was to begin in
two years time. In Jervis's view, and we know Jervis's standards,
he was the finest officer in the Navy, a man of very uncommon
merits, he told the First Lord, 'with honour and courage bright as
his sword'. The commander-in-chief might on occasion question
Nelson's impetuosity; he never doubted Troubridge's capacity.
When he heard of Troubridge's death by drowning in 1807, he was
heard to mutter: 'I shall never see Troubridge's like again. I loved
that invaluable man.'

Edward Berry, a much younger officer than this group, who at
the age of twenty-eight still looked like a boy because of his fair
complexion, was another son of a tradesman. He was Nelson's
first lieutenant in the *Agamemnon*, having joined shortly before they
both transferred to the *Captain*. 'Lt. Berry has joined the ship',
Nelson told his wife. 'He seems a gentleman and an officer from
appearances. I have no doubt but I shall like him.' Soon afterwards
Berry was promoted captain on Nelson's recommendation: 'he is a
protégé of mine and I know him to be an officer of talents, great
courage and laudable ambition'. He was indeed a lion in a fight, both
at the First of June and again at St. Vincent.

The fame of Cuthbert Collingwood, 'my dear Coll', as Nelson
called him after as many years' friendship as with Troubridge, still
lay in the future when he became Nelson's second-in-command at
Trafalgar and then for many years virtually the ruler of the Mediterranean, since he combined his naval position as commander-in-chief
with that of ambassador-at-large. For two and a half years he never
set foot on shore. There never was a man who better exemplified
his own ideal of 'the patient courage which waits for the opportunity
which it cannot create'. 'Old Cuddy' endeared himself to his men
by his consideration for their comfort during the hard conditions
imposed by years of close blockade. In the eyes of posterity, this

5   *The Earl of St. Vincent*
From an engraving by J. R. Smith after G. Stuart, 1797

6   *The captains at the battle of St. Vincent*

From the commemorative engraving by J. Parker and W. N. Worthington after R. Smirke

Top: Earl St. Vincent.
Second row: Sir C. Thompson, Lord Radstock, Sir W. Parker.
Third row: Frederick, Knowles, Collingwood, Whitshed, Lord Nelson, Calder, Dacres, Saumarez, Murray.
Bottom row: Sutton, Troubridge, Martin, Poley, Grey, Towry, Miller, Irwin.

dour-looking North-countryman is the best letter-writer which the Navy has ever produced.

At this date, as captain of the *Excellent*, he was rising fifty. In a less generous-hearted character, one would say that he had a chip on his shoulder. No man had fought with more distinction at the First of June, but in Howe's despatch his name was omitted. We need not go into the reasons here, but when we come to consider Jervis's own despatch we shall see how the slight still rankled. He respected Howe as a seaman, but as he wrote to a friend: 'It would be a sweet sort of revenge to exact from him that justice he has with-held, and if it please God, that day will come.' It came on St. Valentine's day in 1797.

A more barbaric-looking figure was Benjamin Hallowell, the Canadian-born captain of the *Courageux*, a man 'of gigantic frame and vast personal strength'. During the battle he was on board the *Victory*, because his own ship had recently sunk in a gale with the loss of three-quarters of her crew. Ben Hallowell escaped because he happened to be on shore at the time. He looked and spoke like a prize-fighter, but underneath this bear-like exterior Nelson could find 'indefatigable zeal, activity and ability'.

Thomas Foley, now captain of the 100-gun *Britannia* which flew the flag of Vice-Admiral Thompson, was the officer whom Nelson intended to have as his captain of the fleet at Trafalgar, but he was replaced on account of ill health by Thomas Masterman Hardy. Betsy Wynne, wife of Captain Fremantle of the *Inconstant* which was not actually present at the battle, has left us some sketches of Foley when her husband's ship was still in the fleet. 'He is a man between thirty and forty and seems very good natured and gay.' As a lieu-tenant he had served on board the same ship as Prince William, the future William IV or 'Silly Billy'; had not the Prince the good fortune to meet Foley, says a friend, 'his youthful spirits and pro-pensities might not have been checked with such good judgement.' Like Hallowell, he was a giant of a man, over six feet tall, with his hair turning grey, so that Betsy calls him 'the old gentleman'. He spoke rather loud and was fond of naughty stories; but, she adds, he kept an excellent table. He was also a first-rate seaman. It was to his quick judgement that Nelson largely owed the victory of the Nile, for Foley's ship was leading and he was the only captain in the fleet who possessed a chart of Aboukir Bay. Had he not shown the initiative to take the first few ships inside the French line, that victory would certainly not have been so overwhelming.

Foley's ship at the Nile was the *Goliath*, which was also at St. Vincent and even then, according to Jervis, in a disgraceful state of repair. This may have been partly due to her captain at that date, Sir Charles Knowles, of whom Jervis had a very low opinion. Even Betsy Wynne calls him 'a real bore'; Jervis called him 'an imbecile, totally incompetent and the *Goliath* of no use whatsoever under his command'. After the battle Knowles and Foley were told to exchange ships, and the *Britannia* was soon in an equally sad state of discipline, with the crew frequently drunk and disorderly. Yet this son of an admiral ended as Admiral of the Red, the highest rank in the Navy.

Another aristocratic officer was Vice-Admiral William Waldegrave, who flew his flag in the *Barfleur* three-decker, the captain of which was J. B. Dacres. Like Knowles, Waldegrave came of an old naval family, but was much more the 'polished, good-natured gentleman'. There is a pleasant picture of him in the reminiscences of G. S. Parsons, then a twelve-year-old captain's servant doing the duty of a midshipman. The admiral used to let the boy eat as many oranges from his table as he liked, and he always took him around in his barge when he visited other ships. It is odd to reflect how in those days mere children were given responsibility over a tough boat's crew. The boy's spirited account of the battle as it appeared to one of his age will be referred to below. The admiral was created a baronet after the battle and raised to the peerage as Lord Radstock in 1800. He was one of the chief mourners at Nelson's funeral.

Jervis's captain of the fleet was Sir Robert Calder, a man whom Nelson treated with more generosity than he had treated Nelson eight years before his well-known indecisive brush with Villeneuve during the Trafalgar campaign. It was in consequence of this action that he became extremely unpopular at home, so that he begged Nelson's permission to go to England on the eve of Trafalgar to clear his name. Nelson agreed, though it meant weakening his fleet, because he could never refuse the request of 'a brother officer in affliction'. In 1797, however, after the battle of St. Vincent, Calder had mischievously suggested that Nelson's part in the battle was unauthorised. In reply, the Admiral snubbed him severely for his pains.

5

Such were some of the outstanding figures in the Mediterranean fleet. When Spain declared war and her fleet sailed to join that of France at Toulon the autumn before the battle of St. Vincent, a justifiable confidence prevailed, even if the combined fleets outnumbered the British by four to one. 'At home they know not what this fleet is capable of performing, any and *everything*', Nelson told his wife. 'Of all fleets I ever saw, I never saw one in point of officers and men to our present one, and with a commander-in-chief fit to lead them to glory.'

When it was known that Don José de Langara with 19 ships had left Cadiz for Toulon, Nelson wrote from Corsica: 'The Dons are coming up, but in such plight that they cannot stand against our fine fleet, where we are all united. There is nothing our tars look for so earnestly as an opportunity of giving the Dons a total defeat'; and he repeated his opinion that this was the finest fleet 'that ever graced the ocean'.

Though Jervis had more to fear because his responsibilities were the greater, his letters to the First Lord breathe an equally confident tone. It was obvious to him that a fleet so trained and commanded could cut its way through anything. 'Jervis is as firm as a rock', wrote Sir Gilbert Elliot. 'If Man joins him they will certainly fight and they all seem confident of victory.' This was in November, when the fleet was still off Corsica. But the hypochondriacal Man had for some time being begging the Admiralty for leave to return home on the grounds that 'he was an afflicted and unfortunate man, seriously afflicted with a bilious complaint which has chiefly been occasioned by excessive anxiety for the service on which I have been employed'. He had been detached by Jervis to collect provisions at Gibraltar. There the Cadiz fleet brushed past him without trouble and Langara continued to Cartagena to pick up another 7 ships before proceeding to Toulon with 26. Instead of rejoining Jervis, whom he knew to be now heavily outnumbered, Man took the advice of his captains and scuttled back to England.

45

Meanwhile the anxious watchers in the Mediterranean were wearing out their eyes scanning the horizon for the reappearance of Man's squadron. When the news of his defection arrived, Nelson wrote: 'I am surprised that any officer, especially as he thought our force united was too weak to meet the enemy, could desert his brethren; and how he could get English captains to support his measure I am astonished at; yet Man is as good a man and with as upright intentions as ever lived. . . . Our chief is equal to conduct us to honour, and we are equal to obey his wise directions, but he feels Man's retreat severely, says nothing, not even complains of Man, but laments his rash step. I do not believe any officer ever was left in so delicate a situation and few, very few, would have firmness to bear up against it.'

On December 1, 1796, the fleet reached Gibraltar, where Jervis found orders to evacuate the Mediterranean and confine his command to the western coast of the peninsula, making Lisbon his principal rendezvous. The retreat marked not only the lowest point of his fortunes but in the fortunes of the nation as a whole. Holland had been hostile for some time past; Spain and the Italian states were now in alliance with France; our allies had been defeated on the Rhine and on the Po; and now the Mediterranean was closed to our shipping. Five days after Jervis reached Gibraltar the Spanish fleet returned to Cartagena from Toulon and on December 10, Villeneuve, with five French ships of the line, passed the Straits in a gale on his way to Lorient. Everything seemed to be falling into place for a concerted attack on the British Isles. There, a succession of two bad harvests left the country starving. The Bank of England was shortly to refuse payment in cash. Ominous petitions were being forwarded from crews in the Channel fleet, though no one paid any attention to them. More immediately, though this of course was not known, the French were preparing to take the opportunity provided by the Spanish diversion to invade Ireland before the end of the year.

The news of the Bantry Bay fiasco reached Jervis in the middle of January. By that date he had moved from Gibraltar to Lisbon after a disastrous gale had still further weakened his force. Ben Hallowell's *Courageux* was wrecked with the loss of three-quarters of her men. The *Zealous* (74, Captain Samuel Hood) went aground near Tangier. The *Gibraltar* (80, Captain John Pakenham) ran on a reef as she left the bay. Many other ships lost yards and anchors, for Gibraltar was then an open roadstead. In order to repair his damaged fleet and find a safer anchorage, as well as protect Portugal from the threat of invasion from Spain, Jervis moved to the Tagus. Meanwhile, as will be seen, Nelson was detached with two frigates to take off the garrison from the last remaining outpost in the Mediterranean, the isle of Elba.

Jervis entered the Tagus on December 22. Since our minister at Lisbon had failed to provide pilots, and since recent heavy rain had shifted the sandy bottom of the river, the first thing that happened was that the *Bombay Castle* (74) ran aground, and soon afterwards the *St. George* (98) three-decker damaged her bottom on a shoal. Jervis wrote home bitterly: 'the Festivals happening at the moment, the Portuguese were more intent on prayer and rejoicing than in preserving the officers and seamen of the *Bombay Castle*'. The crew was saved by the exertions of other units of the fleet, but the ship was a total loss. The *Gibraltar* had been sent to England for repairs, the *Zealous* and *St. George* were sent into dock to be patched up. Jervis's fine fleet had been reduced in a month from 15 ships to 9.

As if this was not enough, he found the situation at Lisbon even more depressing. He told Spencer that the Government 'exhibits the most melancholy picture I ever read or heard of . . . the commander-in-chief an imbecile . . . the minister of education a bigot . . . an empty treasury . . . crimes go unpunished; honours and rewards bestowed profusely without distinction; the Court filled with monks and friars; and the capital become so offensive, by the dereliction of the police, that it cannot be long without pestilence.' To avoid this, as much as to avoid 'quarrels with the Portuguese which always terminate in assassination', shore leave was strictly limited to the obtaining of provisions and other necessities.

Such was the depressing situation at the opening of the critical year, 1797.

3

Prelude to Battle

THE STRATEGIC AMBITIONS of revolutionary states seldom bear much relation to the military means at their disposal. Having exterminated the officer class, the demagogic leaders of such states trust that doctrinal zeal will outweigh such factors as lack of an administrative machine or even experience in war. On land they have often proved right. The unconventional and highly mobile methods of warfare adopted by Bonaparte in Italy overthrew with astonishing ease the articial systematisation of war which characterised his opponents. But at sea, and more especially in any form of grand strategy involving combined operations such as an invasion scheme, it has been another matter.

We have seen the consequences of the ineptitude of the French attempt to invade Ireland in the depth of winter. An even more extraordinary fiasco was the farcical attempt to invade Wales, which occurred in the same month as the battle of St. Vincent, and to which General Hoche, at least, gave his support. This was the landing of the so-called Black Legion of France at Fishguard under the leadership of an American adventurer who called himself General Tate. Little is known about him, or about the thousand men under his command, except that half of them were convicts. Four French warships put these bandits ashore at Cardigan Bay, but they did not wait to take them off again.

A few hours later Tate's men surrendered to the local Fencibles (as the Home Guard was then called) without firing a shot. They were imprisoned in the church and town hall at Haverfordwest. The story goes that the reason for this pathetic performance was that Tate saw a number of Welshwomen in their tall hats and scarlet cloaks, which he mistook for the uniform of units of the Guards.

What the Directory took far more seriously was a revival of the old scheme of combining the Brest and Toulon fleets to form such a superiority in the Channel that Hoche's army would be able to cross in safety. The plan had been elaborated time and again ever since the start of the French wars in the seventeenth century. It even had certain affinities with the aim of the Spanish Armada. But it never succeeded, either on account of the weather, or on account of the epidemics which invariably broke out on board, or because of the presence of the British fleet. The exceptional difficulty of coordinating sea and land forces remains to this day.

In February 1797 circumstances certainly looked propitious. Ireland was seething with discontent. The British army had done nothing, so far, to enhance a reputation which always stood low on the Continent. The Royal Navy had been excluded from the Mediterranean. In December Admiral Villeneuve had left Toulon and, as we have seen, succeeded in passing the Straits with five ships of the line and three frigates in the same gale which had wrecked so many of Jervis's ships. He was chased into Lorient by units of the Channel fleet and so arrived at Brest too late to take part in the Bantry Bay expedition. But soon after its return he took over the command from Morard de Galles and there were now 30 of the line and 14 frigates concentrated there.

It seemed to the higher command that, now that Spain was in alliance with a very considerable fleet, the Brest ships could be reinforced from Cadiz, as they had been in the similar invasion plan which failed in 1779. De Langara had made his way easily from Cadiz to Toulon: why should he not go in the opposite direction? If a French squadron had passed the Straits, why should not a Spanish?

As we have seen, he did get as far as Cartagena, in company with Villeneuve in December. But while Villeneuve continued through the Straits, the Spanish fleet remained there to refit and prepare themselves for action, to which they were little accustomed. Langara was promoted to a post at Madrid and Don José de Mazaredo was put in command. The French Directory then began to apply pressure to force the Spaniards to sail, but Mazaredo refused to put to sea unless his ships were properly equipped.

Admiral Juan de Cordova (or Cordoba) therefore replaced him.

In compliance with French pressure, he sailed from Cartagena on February 1 with a very poorly manned fleet. It was said that in the flagship herself, the four-decker *Santissima Trinidada* of 136 guns, the largest ship afloat, of which Nelson said 'the *Victory* is nothing to her', there were no more than 60 prime seamen, the rest being landsmen or soldiers, who served both as marines and as gunners. Cordova fought his ship with great courage on the 14th, but the remarkably low standard of seamanship shown by the officers and crews of his ships can only be ascribed to lack of experience. There were few competent captains in the fleet, nor had they experienced anything of the tactical training in which Jervis specialised. There was also a lack of discipline and a correct officer-man relationship which augured certain defeat in battle. After the first enemy broadside the officers lost control of their ships' companies, so that even after men had been flogged or shot as an example, the rest refused to go aloft to set the sails. On several occasions British seamen, peering into the gunports of enemy ships because the action was fought at such close range, swore they saw enemy gun crews quitting their stations as soon as the guns were run out. After the capture of the *San Josef* many tompions were found still in the muzzles of guns which no one had attempted to fire.

Such was the state of Cordova's fleet. The names of his ships and their commanders are printed in the Appendix. In sum, the fleet consisted of one four-decker of 136 guns, 6 three-deckers of 112, 2 two-deckers of 84 and 18 of 74 guns, making a total of 27 line-of-battle ships. There were in addition 12 frigates (Duro, the Spanish naval historian, only lists 8) and 4 large merchant vessels called *urcas* armed with 18–20 guns.

Cordova was not seeking action, because he was only starting on the first stage of a voyage which was to end with the invasion of the British Isles. Such, as we have seen, was the grand strategic objective. But the immediate reason for his passing the Straits on February 5 was quite different and has only recently been appreciated by English naval historians.

This was to convoy four *urcas* laden with mercury from Malaga to Cadiz. In addition to an escort of one three-decker under Vice-Admiral Moreno, the 68-gun ship *San Domingo* was also carrying mercury. This ore came from one of the few mercury mines in

Europe, that at Almaden, 100 miles north of Malaga. Large supplies were required for amalgamating the silver ore from the New World, on which the Spanish and also the French economy now depended. Had Jervis known what was in the ships composing what he called 'the leeward division' of the Spanish fleet, the story of the battle might have been different, though it is doubtful if his tactics would have changed. On the day of battle this division, or van, was separated from the main body, and Jervis acted on the fundamental principle of war that the enemy's main force must be defeated first. It is possible, however, that on the day after the battle, however battered his fleet, he might have loosed his frigates on the *urcas* before they reached Cadiz. As it was, he imagined these large vessels (which he never saw at close range) to be warships in the van and counted them as such in his dispositions throughout the day.

The valuable nature of the convoy helps to explain why Cordova was so anxious to join up with it when it became separated and to cover it with his main body astern. To effect this he had reversed the order of sailing, putting Moreno (hitherto in the rear) in command of the convoy's escorting warships. The confusion which this movement caused before the battle began was one of the reasons for the Spanish defeat, as was the case in Villeneuve's similar change of course before Trafalgar. The lack of seamanship on the part of Cordova's captains and his ability to make them obey or even understand his signals further added to the confusion. However, while the convoy itself stayed safely out of range, Moreno, in the *Principe d'Asturias*, behaved like a good sheep-dog, attacking fiercely whenever his charge was threatened, and by a lucky shot disabling the *Colossus* early in the action.

There was a time early in the present century when an erroneous doctrine prevailed that convoy actions, being so often of a defensive character, were of such an inferior status to fleet actions that they were not worthy of study. But on innumerable occasions a situation has arisen in naval history such as that which occurred on February 14, in which an enemy battle fleet has been brought to action, either from the necessity of guarding a convoy or (as on June 1, 1794) in order to allow its escape. On the latter occasion Howe made the mistake of neglecting a critical grain convoy with far less excuse than Jervis, who never realised that a convoy was involved at all.

Only with the development of submarine warfare in the present century has the convoy become the principle objective of the warship.

The issue at stake on February 14, 1797, was thus not primarily the defeat of a fleet on its way to invade England. But that is what Jervis achieved, and because he achieved it he showed how weak Spanish naval power really was—something which Nelson, for example, never forgot. When the grand strategy of invasion was revived later in the year, it was on the Dutch fleet that the Directory depended, since the Spanish threat had been effectively destroyed by the events which took place on St. Valentine's day.

2

When Nelson received orders at Gibraltar on December 10, 1796, to take off the garrison of the last remaining British outpost in the Mediterranean at Elba, he transferred his commodore's pendant to *La Minerve* (Captain George Cockburn), a fine 38-gun French frigate which had been captured at Toulon. With her sailed the 32-gun frigate *Blanche*. On December 20, off Cartagena, they sighted two large Spanish frigates guarding Cordova's fleet. There followed an action which was harder fought, ship to ship, than any in the fleet action two months later.

The captain of the larger Spanish frigate, the *Sabina* of 40 guns, was Don Jacobo Stuart, a lineal descendant of James II. As the *Minerve* ranged alongside, Nelson hailed him through his speaking trumpet.

'This is an English frigate. If you do not surrender, I will fire.'

'This is a Spanish frigate', replied Stuart stoutly. 'And you may begin as soon as you please.'

'I have no idea of a closer or a sharper battle,' Nelson told his brother when it was over. 'The force to a gun the same, and nearly the same number of men, we having 250. I asked him several times to surrender during the action, but his answer was—'No, Sir, not whilst I have the means of fighting left'. When only himself and his officers were left alive, he hailed and said he would fight no more, and begged that I would stop firing. The next frigate was *La Ceres* of 40 guns, who did not choose to fight much. Not a mast, yard, sail or rope but is hacked to pieces.'

Not one of the Spanish line-of-battle ships at St. Vincent fought like this. Stuart reported 164 men killed, which was more in proportion than the loss on board any single ship in the battle. He himself was brought on board the *Minerve* and generously treated, for Nelson always respected the courage of a spirited opponent. Lieutenants Culverhouse and Hardy were put on board the prize, the *Ceres* having sheered off. On board the *Minerve* there were only seven killed, but the damage sustained left her in a very weak state.

The action proved of no avail. Later in the day a number of big Spanish ships, attracted by the sound of gunfire, appeared in chase of the British frigates and their prize. In the shattered condition the *Minerve* was in, not even Nelson could offer resistance, though normally he would have thought nothing of fighting a frigate against a line-of-battle ship. The prize was cast off, still with her English prize crew on board, and using every shred of what remained of her canvas, the *Minerve* slipped away, only escaping capture through Cockburn's consummate seamanship.

She proceeded to Elba, where Sir Gilbert Elliot and his staff were taken off, though the stubborn old general in command of the garrison refused to budge, in spite of Nelson's succinct explanation of the role of the Navy at this point: 'The object of our fleet in future is the defence of Portugal, and keeping in the Mediterranean the combined fleets.' There was no time for argument. The general was left to his inevitable fate, and the *Minerve* sailed on her return voyage.

Among Elliot's staff was a Colonel John Drinkwater, best known to posterity as the historian of the siege of Gibraltar in the preceeding war. He later took the name of Drinkwater-Bethune and did more than anyone else to heighten, even exaggerate, Nelson's importance at the battle of St. Vincent. When the *Minerve* rejoined Jervis's fleet on the eve of the battle, Elliot and Drinkwater were transferred to the *Lively* frigate, which was on the point of leaving for home with despatches. Since a battle seemed imminent, they begged the admiral to delay her departure until afterwards. Jervis agreed, thus enabling Drinkwater to have a spectator's view of a fleet action in which, as was customary, frigates were not engaged. The result was the best account of the events of February 14 which has come down to us. Drinkwater collated his account with notes made by other participants, notably Nelson (who came on board immediately afterwards, flushed with his first major victory) and then published it anonymously under the title of *A Narrative of the Proceedings of the British Fleet.... By an Officer of H.M. Land Forces.*

In 1840, when it was proposed to erect Nelson's column in Trafalgar Square, Drinkwater decided to publish an enlarged edition, illustrated with small engravings, some of which are reproduced in this book, and to devote the proceeds to the subscription for the monument. In doing so he added everything he could to enhance Nelson's share in the victory, so that succeeding generations have seen the events in a false perspective, with Nelson's dashing courage over-glamorised and Jervis's firmness of mind underestimated.

The *Minerve* reached Gibraltar on February 9. Nelson did not wish to delay, because he heard that units of the Spanish fleet had already sailed to the westward. They had left three line-of-battle ships in the bay, one of which was the *Terrible*, on board of which Hardy and Culverhouse were prisoners. Nelson fully realised the urgency of making contact with Jervis's fleet, but there was just time to effect an exchange of prisoners, as was customary in those more civilised days. Captain Stuart was therefore exchanged for the two English lieutenants and on the evening of February 11 the *Minerve* sped on her way westward.

It was now that Nelson made the acquaintance of the man who is always connected with his name on account of the circumstances of his death. 'Kiss me, Hardy', or as one would prefer to call him, 'Nelson's Hardy', was the captain of the *Victory* at Trafalgar. Now he was merely Lieutenant Thomas Masterman Hardy, aged twenty-seven. He was a big, serene fellow, blunt of speech and uncommonly dull on paper; not very handsome, but 'very superior; the very soul of truth', as a contemporary called him. His devotion to the slightly built Nelson was doglike, not only in admiration of the little man as a leader, but because he saved his life.

No sooner had the *Minerve* slipped her cable and run out from under the protection of the guns on the Rock, than two big Spanish ships anchored further out in the Bay of Algeciras gave chase. The frigate cleared for action, Nelson swearing that he would sooner run her aground than be captured. For the moment the best chance lay in Cockburn's ability to make the most of her sailing qualities. So

Nelson left her in the capable hands of her captain and went below to dinner with Elliot, Drinkwater and Hardy.

The latter was just being congratulated on being no longer a prisoner when there was a cry of 'Man overboard!' The officers ran up on deck, while the passengers thronged to peer through the stern windows of the captain's cabin. A jolly-boat was lowered and Hardy jumped in, but in a moment the strong current running through the Straits carried her astern towards the Spanish ships. It was too late to save the drowning man. As the boat crew strained at their oars, it became increasingly clear that they were being carried down upon the enemy. 'By God, I'll not lose Hardy!' cried Nelson on the quarter-deck. 'Back the mizen topsail!'

The frigate's way was checked. The boat's crew pulled harder than before. Action seemed imminent, as the leading Spanish ship slowly closed the gap between her and the frigate. But at that moment the Spanish captain lost his nerve. Knowing that Nelson was on board, he wanted to allow his consort to catch up with him before engaging too closely. He, too, shortened sail, and in the precious minutes of respite which this provided, Hardy's boat was able to get alongside the *Minerve*. The boat was hauled on board, studding-sails spread and the frigate began to draw away again from her pursuers. By nightfall they were out of sight.

4

The Battle of St Vincent

FROM TIME IMMEMORIAL mariners rounding Cape St. Vincent
have saluted the headland, the most westerly point of the continent
of Europe, by lowering their topsails. It was from his palace at Sagres,
on this cape, that Prince Henry the Navigator watched the sails of
his explorers' ships disappear below the horizon on their way south
to discover the unknown coastline of Africa in the first phase of
European expansion. Ever since, the strategic importance of the
cape, lying as it does between the Straits of Gibraltar and the ports
on the Atlantic seaboard, has been marked by the number of battles
which have been fought in its vicinity. Trafalgar, which took place
only 100 miles south-east of St. Vincent, was but the last of a long
series, and it is significant that the Americans have chosen Rota, near
Cadiz, which lies between the two capes, as their chief base in Europe
today.

After singeing the King of Spain's beard at Cadiz in 1587, Drake
sacked Lagos, the chief port on the promontory of St. Vincent. In
the eighteenth century there were half a dozen actions hereabouts,
as French or Spanish squadrons emerged from the Mediterranean in
order to concentrate their forces on the Atlantic seaboard. In a
strategic situation which closely resembles that of 1797, Boscawen
drove the ships of De La Clue ashore at Lagos in the year 1759,
when the French fleet was attempting to unite with that at Brest for
the purpose of invading the British Isles. In 1780 Rodney had
defeated Langara himself here in the Moonlight Battle, the only
night action on a big scale to be fought before the battle of Matapan.
On that occasion Rodney had twice the number of ships as his
opponents, and the battle had taken the form of a chase. Now Jervis
had only half the enemy force; but, as he said, 'It is men, not ships,

that win battles.' And he knew that he could trust the fleet which he had trained to fight against any odds.

For this reason he was determined not to stay longer at Lisbon than the necessities of revictualling required, 'inaction in the Tagus will make us all cowards'. The first startling news that reached him was on January 8, when he heard that the French were out of Brest and was warned that they might be heading south, for such as we have seen, had been Pellew's guess. Actually they had gone west to Bantry Bay, but the news persuaded Jervis that it was his duty to escort a Portuguese convoy bound for Brazil out into the Atlantic. He did not intend to see it far beyond the latitude of Cape St. Vincent, because he daily expected the return of Nelson with news of the Spanish fleet, last heard of at Cartagena. He therefore left Lisbon on January 18 with the intention of reaching his rendezvous in a few days, but contrary winds delayed him so long that he did not get there until February 6.

There he found not only Lord Garlies with the frigates which he had left to cruise in the neighbourhood of Cadiz in order to give him warning of the approach of the Spaniards, but the long-awaited reinforcements under Rear-Admiral Sir William Parker—the *Prince George*, *Namur*, *Orion*, *Irresistible*, *Colossus* and *Thalia* frigate.

The Parker who flew his flag in the *Prince George* is not to be confused with other admirals of the same name, Hyde Parker, for instance, of Copenhagen fame. He was a sound, if somewhat pompous, senior officer, who was one of the few who ever dared to criticise Nelson. Jervis placed his division in the van on the day of battle because Parker's ships, recently out of England, were the fastest and soundest in his fleet. Among their captains, the man who was to play the most important part in the battle was Sir James Saumarez, another touchy and ceremonious character, whom Nelson never liked. He came of a distinguished Guernsey family long connected with the Navy, the members of which never had any trouble to press men for their ships because they could always man them with Channel Island volunteers. Betsy Fremantle called him 'the civilest man' she ever met; but this was hardly a compliment because his manner was too formal to be friendly. Since he did not think he received his deserts for his services at St. Vincent, he always had a chip on his shoulder, even after his handling of affairs in the Baltic during the last years of the war proved him to be one of the best sailor-diplomatists that England has ever had.

'I thank you very much for sending so good a batch', Jervis told the First Lord on the arrival of such badly needed reinforcements. 'They are a valuable addition to my excellent stock.' But that stock even after their arrival only amounted to 15 ships of the line (of which 6, indeed, were three-deckers), besides 4 frigates, a sloop and a cutter. Though Jervis was ignorant of the exact number of the enemy, Cordova's fleet actually amounted to 27 of the line (of which the *Santissima Trinidada* was a four-decker and no less than 6 others were three-deckers) 10 frigates and a brig, apart from the 4 big *urcas* in the convoy. In fire-power, the Spanish were almost exactly twice as strong as the British, had all their ships been present at the battle.

On the other hand, as we have seen, Jervis's ships were infinitely better trained and in the days preceding the battle he had made admirable use of his frigates as an early warning system. They had been left cruising off Cadiz for the past month with orders to notify him at a rendezvous off Cape St. Vincent. This they tried to do, but so small was the main fleet and so difficult was it in those days to determine a position at sea accurately, that it was often impossible for them to find him. Thus the fast-sailing frigate *La Bonne Citoyenne*, sighted the Spaniards on February 8 ninety miles south-east of the rendezvous, but could not discover where the admiral was on her return.

Hence it was later that day the first news reached him by a cutter from Gibraltar that the Spaniards were on their way. A strong wind, or Levanter, continued to blow from the east, carrying Cordova much further out into the Atlantic than he had intended on his way to Cadiz. Jervis was lying snug under the lee of the Cape, well placed to intercept him and when the *Emerald* frigate confirmed the cutter's news on February 10 he told the Admiralty, 'I flatter myself we shall be able to deal with them.'

But the bad luck which had been pursuing him for the past two months had not yet run out. Soon after he heard news of Cordova's approach, the *Colossus* collided with the *Culloden* in the middle of the night. Troubridge's ship was badly damaged, her jib boom and fore topmast carried away and her bowsprit split. Another captain might well have asked permission to return to port, but a battle seemed

7   *Nelson boarding the 'San Josef'*
From a mezzotint by J. Daniell after H. Singleton

8 The 'Captain' (centre) engaging the 'San Nicolas' (right) and 'San Josef' (left)
From a painting by R. Dodd

imminent and Troubridge was not the man to miss one. By extraordinary exertions his crew made the *Culloden* fit for service the next
day, and it was only right that he was given the honour of leading
the line on the day of battle.

The *Emerald* was sent off again to resume contact with the enemy,
but, like others, she failed to find the admiral on her return. This
time the *Bonne Citoyenne* was more fortunate and reported the close
presence of the enemy on February 13.

This was also the day Nelson arrived in the *Minerve* and now Jervis's
luck changed for the better.

The commodore was able to tell him that he had sighted the
enemy battle fleet seventeen leagues away on the 11th, and had indeed
sailed right through them in the night. He had woken Drinkwater
up with the news that the frigate seemed to be surrounded by much
larger ships, though thick weather made it impossible to say how
many or what they were. The two officers decided not to wake Sir
Gilbert Elliot until dawn, but the sound of their voices roused the
old man from his bed. It was agreed that they would stretch away
to the westward, if necessary to the West Indies, should morning
light reveal that the enemy lay between them and the British fleet.
However, at daylight on the 12th nothing was seen of the phantom
fleet, because the strong Levanter which carried Cordova through
the Straits had blown his ships far to the westward. Only when the
wind veered to the south of west was it possible for the Spaniards
to alter course ESE in the direction of Cadiz.

Having given his commander-in-chief this intelligence, and having
put his passengers on board the *Lively* frigate, Nelson transferred
his pennant to the 74-gun *Captain*. Captain Miller piped him over
the side, with the young Berry standing apart, resplendent in a new
captain's uniform after his recent promotion on Nelson's recommendation.

That evening Jervis gave a dinner party on board the *Victory* in
honour of Sir Gilbert Elliot, Captain Hallowell being also present
because his ship had been wrecked a few weeks previously and he
was now a passenger on board the flagship. Elliot begged the
admiral to delay the departure of the *Lively* for England since
action seemed imminent, and Jervis agreed; but when the Governor
suggested that he might be allowed to remain on board the flagship

he refused permission, because he did not want any civilians on his quarter-deck should an engagement take place. So, after a toast had been drunk—'Victory over the Dons in the battle which they cannot escape tomorrow'—Elliot and Drinkwater were rowed back to their frigate.

Cordova was just as anxious that a battle should take place, although initially he had not sought one. A few days earlier he had been informed by an American neutral that Jervis had only nine ships of the line. But this was just before Parker's ships arrived and the *Culloden* had joined from the southward. Instead of trusting to crush Jervis by weight of numbers, Cordova therefore had an unpleasant surprise when he saw the situation on the morning of February 14.

The previous night Jervis had taken all precautions against what the morning light might reveal. The frigates were disposed as scouts for the main fleet, and the signal 'Prepare for battle' had been sent out to all ships of the line, with orders to sail in close order during the hours of darkness. Curiously enough, some ships seem to have been seen slow in their preparations. Quite late the next morning we find the master of the *Orion* sadly noting in his log that because of delay in clearing ship, 100 water barrels, 180 hogsheads, 250 puncheons and spare stores such as canvas berths, tables, bread bags and butt staves had to be thrown overboard in haste.

At 2.30 on the morning of the 14th, Cape St. Vincent bearing twenty-four miles NE, a Scotsman who was in command of a Portuguese frigate gave Jervis the information that the Spanish fleet was fifteen miles away to windward, course ESE, a light, variable wind now blowing from the south-west. At 5.30 Lieutenant Foote of the *Niger* frigate joined with news that they were even closer. He had made contact with them soon after the *Bonne Citoyenne* had left on the 13th and had searched all night for the British fleet, only to find them at dawn. At 6.30 the *Victory*'s log states: 'Discovered a number of strange sail to windward, supposed to be the Spanish fleet', but the thick morning mist did not permit more detailed information.

The commander-in-chief had not slept that night. He sat up writing his will until the sound of the enemy's signal guns drew him from his cabin to the quarter deck at dawn. All that he could see through the mist was the close order in which his own fleet still sailed after

the difficulty of keeping station at night. Their order was so gratifying that he signalled his approbation to the captains, adding in
full realisation of the political importance of the coming encounter:
'A victory is very essential to England at this moment.'

It was far otherwise with Cordova. His fleet was in no sort of order,
though there was little sea running and hardly any wind. The convoy
and its escort was separated from the main body a long way to
leeward. Cordova tried to close it up, but his signals could not be
seen till later in the morning. He was trying to form close order to
keep the weather gauge, but even when his signals were received
three of his largest ships, in their anxiety to obey, fell so far to
leeward that they never took their place in the line. These were the
Principe d'Asturias, Oriente and *Regla*, and two of them were commanded by Vice-Admirals—Moreno and Amblimont. Thus Cordova's
fleet, originally 27 in number, was now reduced to 17, three ships of
the line having been left behind at Algeciras, two having been
ordered to the southward, and now five warships were lying well
to leeward of the enemy, together with the convoy. Since two of
his admirals were thus out of the action from the start (though
Moreno did his best to join later on) and most of his remaining
senior officers were stationed in the rear when the admiral ordered
the ships to form line, the rest were as sheep without a shepherd.

As the mist lifted Jervis could see the gap between the two
bodies. He decided at first to stand towards the leeward group. The
Culloden and five of Parker's ships were ordered to chase, and when
the *Citoyenne* signalled more ships in that quarter, they were reinforced.
But at that moment the *Minerve* signalled that the main body was
to windward; at first 16 ships, then 25, were reported to be in sight.

As captain of the fleet, Calder gave the admiral the news as it came
in. 'There are eight sail of the line, Sir John.'

'Very well, Sir.'

'There are twenty sail of the line, Sir John.'

'Very well, Sir.'

'There are twenty-five sail of the line, Sir John.'

'Very well, Sir.'

'There are twenty-seven sail, Sir John.'

'Enough, Sir, no more of that: the die is cast, and if there are
fifty sail I will go through them.'

'That's right, Sir John', exclaimed the gigantic Hallowell, as he slapped the admiral's back in his excitement. 'That's right, by God we shall give them a damned good licking.'

At 11.0 Jervis signalled to form line of battle ahead or astern of the flagship, as most convenient, on a course bearing SSW, thus recalling the ships which had been sent to chase the leeward division. But these had already achieved their aim by making the convoy and its escort turn away, with the exception of one ship which continued to bear up towards the main body. This was the *San Ysidro*, which now wore to stand on the other tack in order to pass astern of the British. She was a two-decker, but as she passed the *Lively* frigate the latter's master-gunner begged Lord Garlies to let him take a shot at her with his favourite 18-pounder gun. The captain agreed, though normally frigates never dared to interfere with big ships. The shot struck the *San Ysidro* amidships, killing five men, but the two-decker continued on her course, giving the frigate a broadside as she passed. However, the aim of the Spanish gunners was so high that not a shot hit the hull, though many went through the rigging. It was particularly gratifying to the *Lively*'s crew that after the capture of the *San Ysidro* later in the day, she was the frigate which was told to take her in tow.

His line now formed, at 11.29 Jervis signalled his intention 'to pass through the enemy line', that is to say through the gap between the convoy or leeward division, and Cordova's main body. In contrast to the admirably close-hauled British line, Cordova laments in his despatch that in attempting to form his own line, three ships fell off at leeward and many others misunderstood his intentions, so that no real line was ever formed, the Spanish ships lying three or four abreast in an ungainly bunch.

At 11.30 the *Culloden* leading the line opened fire as she passed through the gap. (See Plan I, p. 65). The first lieutenant told Troubridge that there must be a collision if they stayed on the same course. 'Can't help it, Griffiths', the captain replied, 'let the weakest fend off.' So close did the two ships pass that the English crew could peer into the other's gunports and their broadside struck with such effect that they could see the enemy ship shudder visibly, even though all the guns on one side of a ship were never fired simultaneously because of the strain on the timbers. When we speak of a

Plan I

**Battle of
ST. VINCENT
1130 a.m.
February 14, 1797**

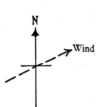

N

Wind

B

A

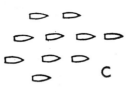

D

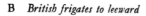

C

A *British fleet in line of battle*	C *Main body of Spanish fleet to wind-ward*
B *British frigates to leeward*	D *Spanish van and convoy to leeward*

broadside what we really mean is a ripple of shot from bow to stern as each gun is fired in succession. An observer of the *Culloden*'s broadside on this occasion speaks of the guns as fired 'as if by a seconds-watch and in the silence of a port-admiral's inspection'. Moreover, even a double-shotted broadside fired at close range was insufficient to sink a wooden ship, unless an explosion followed, because solid shot simply passed through the hull of such a ship. However, on this occasion the Spaniard received such a kick in the face that she went about without being able to fire a shot in reply.

Seeing that the British line now lay between him and his leeward division, Cordova now altered course in order to pass astern of Jervis's fleet. The morning mist having lifted, the *Culloden*, *Prince George*, *Orion* and *Colossus* were all engaged so fiercely with the enemy's rear ships that smoke prevented Jervis from seeing what was happening. When he realised Cordova's intention, he decided at 12.8 to order his whole line to tack in succession in order to engage the enemy on the same tack, and this time to pass through him (or rather inside him, because the Spanish ships lay two or three abreast) from to windward instead of from to leeward. The situation and the order of the British ships of the line is shown on the Plan II, p. 67.

The *Victory*'s log states broadly that 'at 12.15 the action became general from van to centre [i.e. from the *Culloden* to the *Victory*]. At noon the fleet engaging the enemy on different tacks. Employed passing through the enemy and engaging to windward.' If the Spanish lee division had made any attempt to engage at this juncture, the British would have been between two fires, but once Jervis's ships were embroiled among Cordova's it was too late. The main body was, indeed, as formless as a flock of sheep, and all that the ships composing it could now do was to follow their towering flagship in her effort to pass astern of the British line.

There was, however, one exception to the failure of the lee division to engage. Instead of wearing before the wind, as did the rest of his ships, Vice-Admiral Joaquin Moreno in the *Principe d'Asturias* (112 guns) held on towards the *Victory* of almost the same size. A collision seemed imminent until Moreno, within pistol-shot of the British flagship, suddenly lost his nerve and turned away by putting his helm down and merely saluting his adversary with a few

Plan II

ST. VINCENT
1208

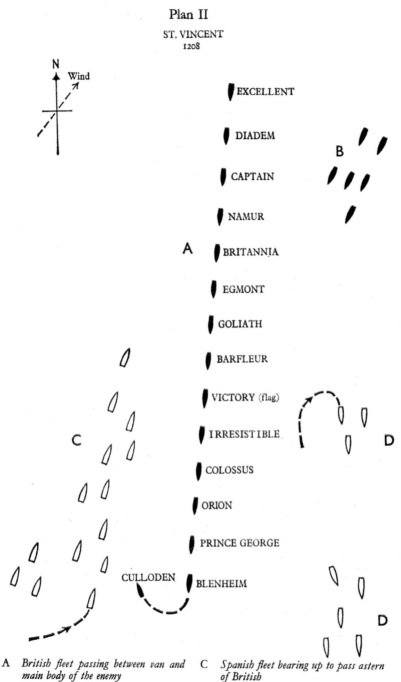

N Wind

EXCELLENT

DIADEM

B

CAPTAIN

NAMUR

A BRITANNIA

EGMONT

GOLIATH

BARFLEUR

VICTORY (flag)

IRRESISTIBLE

C

COLOSSUS D

ORION

PRINCE GEORGE

CULLODEN BLENHEIM

D

A British fleet passing between van and
   main body of the enemy

B British frigates

C Spanish fleet bearing up to pass astern
   of British

D Spanish van wearing and falling away
   to leeward

starboard guns. As the ship swung round she offered an open target for the *Victory* to rake her with a thunderous broadside. In a moment her deck was a shambles, her steering wheel shot away, her rudder jammed, so that she turned a full circle just in time to receive another shattering broadside on her starboard side. Reeling under this double blow, she fell away to leeward and took no further part in the action. 'Raked her both ahead and astern', says the *Victory*'s log; 'he appeared to be in great confusion and bore up, as did other of the enemy ships.'

So intelligently did Troubridge anticipate Jervis's signal to tack in succession that before the flags fluttered out on board the flagship his own acknowledgement signal was ready to be broken at the top-gallant mast of the *Culloden*. 'Break the stop—Down with the helm!' he shouted, and the ship swung round on the opposite tack. Accustomed as he was to the highest standards of seamanship, Jervis could not restrain his delight at Troubridge's virtuosity. 'Look', he cried to the master of the *Victory*, 'Look at Troubridge there! He tacks his ship in battle as if the eyes of England were upon him; and would to God they were, for they would see him to be, what I know him to be, and, by Heaven, sir, as the Dons will soon feel him to be!'

The other van ships followed the *Culloden* with the same skilful promptitude, all except the *Colossus* which, losing a foresail yard from a chance shot from Moreno's ship, missed stays and swerved heavily across the *Irresistible* astern of her. In turn, the *Victory* had to back her main topsail to avoid a collision. The *Colossus* then fell out of the line and took no further part in the battle; indeed, by the end of it she had become a liability.

About this time, as the British van began to fall in among the Spanish rear, a shot took off the head of a marine standing beside Jervis on the quarter-deck, covering the admiral from head to foot with the man's blood and brains. Fearing that the admiral was wounded, the captain of marines ran up. 'I am not at all hurt', replied Jervis, wiping the blood off his face, 'but do, George, try if you can get me an orange.' A midshipman ran up with one from the cockpit and Jervis rinsed his mouth with it. As soon as he had done so, he ordered Signal 41 to be hoisted—to take suitable stations for mutual support and to engage the enemy more closely. In other

Plan III

ST. VINCENT
1300

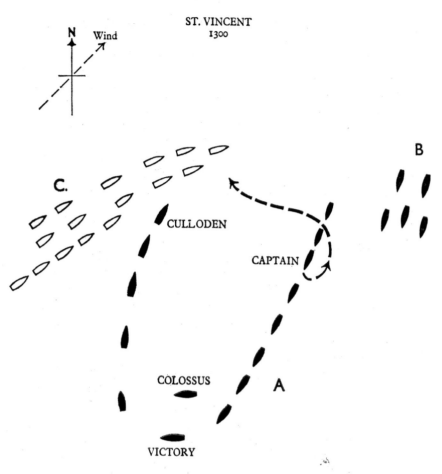

A *British fleet, with 'Captain' wearing out of the line and 'Colossus' disabled*

B *British frigates*

C *Spanish fleet led by 'S. Trinidada', 'S. Nicolas' and 'S. Josef'*

D *Spanish van*

words, in the smoke and confusion of the battle he left his van ships to their own devices, trusting that his rear would close up in support as best they could. Gone was the strict formation of the line of battle, which up to this moment had served its purpose so admirably; now the form of tactics to be employed was left to the initiative of individual captains.

Cordova was now attempting to pass astern of the British line (see Plan III, p. 69). When Jervis ordered his ships to tack in succession in order to follow him, it was obvious to Nelson in the *Captain*, lying third from the rear, that, by the time the whole British line had turned, the Spanish admiral would have achieved his aim, because he had the advantage of the wind. At one o'clock, therefore, he told Miller to wear the ship out of the line in order to stand on the other tack himself and thereby anticipate the Spanish move. As the log states: 'The Commodore ordered the ship to be wore; when passing between the *Diadem* and *Excellent* [the two ships astern of her], she was immediately engaged with the *Santissima Trinidada* and two other three-deck ships, in which we were nobly supported by the *Culloden*.' The adjective in the last sentence suggests that the commodore himself dictated it.

By throwing this ship, although only a 74, across the path of the 136-gun Spanish flagship and the three-deckers astern of her, Nelson forced them to alter course, thus giving Jervis's ships time to work their way further into the main body. Only a tactician of genius, certain of his own judgement, and only a man utterly without fear, would have dared to do this. Because of what followed, posterity can hardly be blamed for ascribing the victory to him; but it is well to recall that the van had been in action, thanks to Jervis's determination, for over an hour before Nelson's manœuvre delivered the *coup-de-grâce*. As has been seen, the *Culloden* was heading for the same ships at the same time as the *Captain* came up on her own. Was it an act of selfish disobedience to the signal flying on board the flagship, or was it a brilliant example of initiative?

Nothing succeeds like success. Had Nelson failed and had the *Captain* been dismasted at the start, he might well have been court-martialled. But he did not fail, as he might equally have done when in the *Victory* he met the same *Santissima Trinidada* on the morning of Trafalgar, because he intuitively assessed the chances of destruc-

Plan IV

ST. VINCENT
1500

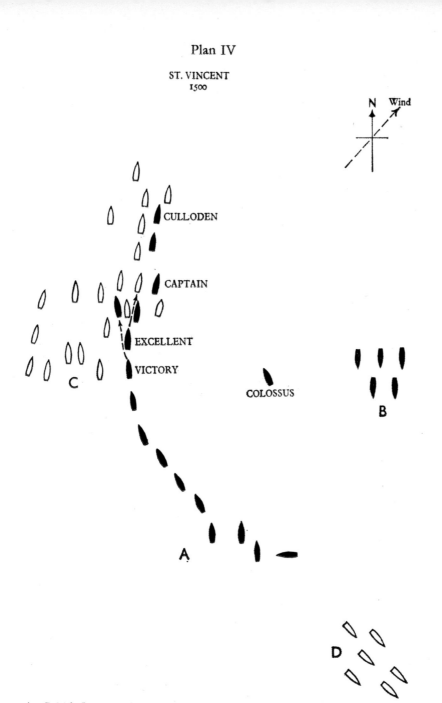

A   *British fleet engaged: 'Captain' with 'S. Nicolas' and 'S. Josef'; 'Excellent' with 'S. Ysidro'; 'Culloden' and van ships with 'S. Trinidada', etc.; 'Victory' with 'S. Salvador'*

B   *British frigates*

C   *Spanish main body*

D   *Spanish van*

tion with the inevitable rewards of success. Surely Mahan's comment settles the issue: 'In this well-timed, but most daring move, which illustrates to the highest degree the immense difference between a desperate and a reckless action, Nelson passed to the head of the British column, crossing the bows of five large Spanish vessels, and with his 74 engaged the *Santissima Trinidada* of 136 guns, the biggest ship at that time afloat.'

It was thus that a comparatively obscure commodore sailed into history. The ships which the *Captain* now engaged were the *Trinidada*, closely supported by the *San Josef* of 112 guns, the *Salvador del Mundo* of 112 and the *San Nicolas* of 80. Fortunately, the *Culloden* was nearly up with the latter, having fought her way through the ships astern, and Collingwood's *Excellent*, the rearmost ship in the British line, was prompt to follow his friend's example in wearing out of the line. Within a few moments of the preposterous spectacle of a two-decker engaging a four-decker, there were three ships in support of her—*Culloden, Excellent, Blenheim*—and the rest of Parker's ships were not far away. For the next hour the battle was a melée. (See Plan IV, p. 71.) According to Parker, 'we sometimes had the fire of two or three ships together; yet from their disordered state, our fire had great effect upon them, for it could not be lost; they were generally so huddled together in a very irregular manner, and I have no doubt but that they did each other a great deal of injury.'

'It is a very difficult thing for anyone, particularly one who is engaged, to relate the circumstances of a battle', wrote Collingwood after the action. 'Everyone is so much employed by attention to his own situation and watching the movements and signals of the Admiral, that it is impossible to know exactly what others are doing. . . . The truth is, we did not proceed on any system of tactics. In the beginning we were formed very close and pushed at them without knowing, through the thickness of the haze, with what part of the line we could fall in. When they were divided, and the lesser part driven to leeward, the Admiral wisely abandoned them, made the signal to tack, and afterwards stuck to the larger divisions of the fleet, which was to windward, and could not be joined by the lee division in a short time. After this we had neither order nor signals, for the Admiral was so satisfied with the impetuosity of the attack made by the ships ahead of him that he let us alone.'

9   The 'Victory' (centre) engaging the 'San Salvador' (right) off Cape St. Vincent
From a coloured aquatint by C. Rosenberg after W. J. Huggins

10   *The British van engaging the main body of the Spanish fleet at the battle of St. Vincent*
From a painting by R. Dodd

11   *Nelson boarding the 'San Nicolas'*

No wonder that the blow-by-blow account left by the school-master of the *Excellent* makes confusing reading. Poor Christie had been told by Collingwood to note down the signals during the action—'an unpleasant station, I assure you: it is not easy in the heat of action to write with composure. I will fairly tell you I could not then have solved a problem in the Mathematicks.' After noting the Admiral's signal to engage closer, all he could write was: 'made more sail, bore up and ran between a Spanish two-decker and a three-decker, commenced a smart fire on the three-decker, who soon struck [this must have been the *Salvador del Mundo*]. At 2.40 our own ships to leeward firing over us, as we came into their line of fire. The Admiral made the signal to discontinue the engagement. Set our mainsail and ran close alongside a two-deck ship. At 2.50 engaged the two-decked ship [*San Ysidro*] and at 3.0 she surrendered and struck her colours to the British flag.'

Collingwood's letter to his wife is more specific: 'The first ship we engaged was the *San Salvador del Mundo* of 112 guns, a first rate; we were not further from her when we began than the length of our garden. Her colours soon came down, and her fire ceased. I hailed and asked if they surrendered; and when by signs made by a man who stood by the colours I understood they had, I left her to be taken possession of by somebody behind, and made sail for the next, but was very much surprised on looking back to find her colours up again, and the battle recommenced. We very soon came up with the next, the *San Ysidro*, 74, so close alongside that a man might jump from one ship to the other. Our fire carried all before it; and in ten minutes she hauled down her colours; but I had been deceived once, and obliged this fellow to hoist English colours before I left him, and made a signal for somebody behind to board him, when the Admiral ordered the *Lively* frigate to take charge of him. Then making all sail, passing between our line and the enemy, we came up with the *San Nicolas*, of 80 guns, which happened at the time to be abreast of the *San Josef*, of 112 guns; we did not touch sides, but you could not put a bodkin between us, so that our shot passed through both ships, and in attempting to extricate themselves they got on board each other. My good friend, the Commodore, had been long engaged with these ships, and I came happily to his relief, for he was dreadfully mauled. Having engaged them until their fire ceased on me, though their colours were not down, I went on to the *S. Trinidada* of 132 guns on four complete decks—such a ship as I never saw before. By this time our masts, sails and rigging were so much shot about that we could not get so near to her as I would have been; but near enough to receive much injury from her, both in my men and ship. We were engaged an hour with this ship, and trimmed her well; she was a complete wreck.'

Nelson's account of his experience in the *Captain*, which he wrote for the benefit of the Duke of Clarence whom he had known as a midshipman, is far less consecutive, but full of generous remarks about being 'nobly supported' by Troubridge, and how Collingwood 'gallantly pushed up, with every sail set, to save his old friend and messmate'. It is only after Collingwood's fire had forced the *San Josef* to fall on board the *San Nicolas* that the details emerge clearly:

'At this time the *Captain*, having lost her foretop mast, not a sail shroud or rope left, her wheel shot away, and incapable of further service in the line, or in chase, I ordered Captain Miller to put the helm a-starboard and calling for boarders, ordered them to board.*

'The soldiers of the 69th Regiment [who were serving on board in the capacity of marines] with an alacrity which will ever do them credit, and Lieutenant Pierson of the same Regiment, were among the foremost in this service. The first man who jumped into the enemy's mizzen chains was Captain Berry, late my First Lieutenant; Captain Miller was in the very act of going also, but I directed him to remain.†

'He was supported from our spritsail yard, which hooked into the mizzen rigging. A soldier having broke the upper quartergallery window, jumped in, followed by myself and others as fast as possible. I found the cabin door fastened, and some Spanish

---

* The editor of Nelson's *Letters and Despatches* dismisses the story that the Commodore led the way with the cry 'Westminster Abbey or Glorious Victory' as a 'gasconade very inconsistent with his character'. But since much the same remark was made at the Nile, and as Drinkwater reports it in his first, though not in his second edition, we may accept it as typical.

† Miller's sister says that Nelson's words were: 'No, Miller, I must have that honour.' After the action he presented Miller with the sword of the Spanish Captain and a topaze ring, saying 'Miller, I am under the greatest obligations to you.'

officers fired their pistols; but having broke open the doors, the soldiers fired, and the Spanish Brigadier or Commodore fell, as retreating to the quarter deck, near the wheel. Having pushed on to the quarter deck, I found Captain Berry in possession of the poop, and the Spanish ensign hauling down. I passed with my people and Lieutenant Pierson on to the larboard gangway to the forecastle, where I met two or three Spanish officer prisoners to my seamen, and they delivered me their swords.

'At this moment a fire of pistols or muskets opened from the admiral's stern gallery of the *San Josef*. I directed the soldiers to fire into her stern; and calling to Captain Miller ordered him to send more men into the *San Nicolas*, and directed my people to board the first-rate, which was done in an instant, Captain Berry assisting me into the main chains. At this moment a Spanish officer looked over from the quarter-deck rail and said they surrendered; from this most welcome intelligence it was not long before I was on the quarter-deck, where the Spanish Captain, with a bow, presented me his sword, and said the Admiral was dying of his wounds below. I asked him, on his honour, if the ship were surrendered? He declared she was; on which I gave him my hand and desired him to call his officers and ship's company to tell them of it, which he did; and on the quarter-deck of a Spanish first-rate, extravagant as the story may seem, did I receive the swords of vanquished Spaniards; which, as I received, I gave to William Fearney, one of my bargemen, who put them with the greatest sangfroid under his arm.'

Such was 'Nelson's Patent Bridge for Boarding First-Rates', as it became known. Daniel Orme's picture, reproduced as fig. 4, represents the climax of the story on board the *San Josef* with such literalness that he printed a key to it. Standing to the right of the picture, on Nelson's left, is Berry. On Nelson's right, Lieutenant Pierson in his red military uniform is informing Nelson that the Spanish captain, Don Jose Delkenna, is surrendering the sword of the expiring admiral, Don F. Z. Winthuysen, who, having lost both legs, was actually below deck at this moment, but who is here shown in the left-hand corner of the picture. Captain Miller and Nelson's stepson, Josiah, together with a sailor in a white shirt may be dimly discerned in the background on the poop of the *Captain* behind the figurehead of a lion, into whose jaws has been thrust a captured ensign. Lieutenant Withers is seen speaking to the Spanish chaplain. In the right-hand corner is a British seaman called Hopper, who struck the Spanish colours, and on the left, kneeling beside the dying admiral, is William Fearney, who received the surrendered swords. He was a native of Nelson's own village in Norfolk. The bell of the *San Josef* is now hung at the Navy's training establishment, H.M.S. *Ganges*, in Suffolk.

The fame of this story has obscured the real crux of the battle, which was the hour-long struggle between the *Culloden* and the ships astern of her with the main body of the Spanish fleet. As Cordova admits in his despatch, the way they fought 'in great good order, with a heavy and well directed fire, decided the action in their favour'. Five Spanish ships received the brunt of the British attack—*Santissima Trinidada*, *Salvador del Mundo* (which surrendered), and Nelson's two prizes, *San Nicolas* and *San Josef*; there was also the *Mexicano*, which got off lightest.

The Spanish flagship sustained the heaviest damage of all, having been attacked, says Cordova, 'the whole afternoon by a three-decker and three ships of 74 guns that raked her fore and aft at pistol shot; and notwithstanding her having upwards of 200 men killed and wounded, she still continued the action for a full hour longer'. For their part, the British were convinced that at one point in the afternoon she surrendered to Saumarez in the *Orion*, but Cordova of course does not mention this.

Saumarez's account of his achievements (for which he thought he never received due recognition, and certainly not in the narrative of the man he calls 'our desperate Commodore') is that the *Orion* first engaged the *Salvador del Mundo* before the latter struck to the *Victory*, though a boat's crew from his ship was allowed to take possession. Lieutenant Luce, in charge of the prize crew, found fifty Spanish wounded lying on the upper deck in need of amputation. The surgeon had operated on a number of others, but had failed to tie up arteries, relying in his haste on the efficacy of tourniquets. The British sailors regarded this as plain inhumanity and threatened to throw the man overboard. It must be added that Luce was later dismissed for allowing his party to pilfer the ship.

The *Orion* then moved up against the *Santissima Trinidada*, which, says Saumarez, clearly surrendered to her by first showing a white flag and then the British flag over the Spanish colours. At this the *Orion* ceased fire. But at the same moment the *Victory* signalled the whole fleet to wear in order to protect the *Captain* and *Collossus*. Saumarez had therefore to abandon what would have been the richest prize of all and had the mortification of seeing the ship resume Spanish colours.

After the battle was over Nelson said in his effusive way, 'It was true, Saumarez, that the *Santissima* struck to you: the Spanish officers confirm it.'

'Who ever doubted it, Sir?' replied Saumarez abruptly. 'I hope there is no need for such evidence to establish the truth of a report of a British officer.'

Nevertheless, the incident was not reported in Jervis's despatch, nor was the name of Saumarez mentioned.

By five o'clock the short February day was waning. For the first time the Spanish lee division showed signs of fight, though what they were really doing was protecting the *Santissima Trinidada* as she staggered out of the melée before the wind. Jervis saw that if he was to secure his prizes and succour the crippled *Captain* it was necessary to break off action. He therefore ordered his ships to form line astern of the *Victory* and told the frigates to take the prizes in tow. (See Plan V, p. 82.)

Cordova interprets the move thus: 'The enemy, observing our van standing towards them, immediately retired together, covering the captured ships.' He ascribes his defeat to the fact that the British were 'in a readier condition to form line of battle at the start than could be performed by our squadron', because of the necessity of protecting the convoy—a thin excuse for the low standard of seamanship and tactical discipline evinced by his captains throughout the action. Only 17 of his 27 ships ever attempted to form line, and then in a loose and hasty formation. Of those 17, the majority never had the opportunity to fire, the enemy's attack being concentrated on some half dozen ships, of which four were captured.

As for the flagship, at the end of the day Cordova describes her as 'entirely dismasted, without the power of making signals with flags or lights'. The admiral says that he considered the wisdom of renewing action the next day, since he still had more ships than the enemy, but on enquiring into the state of his fleet he found three

Plan V

ST. VINCENT
1700

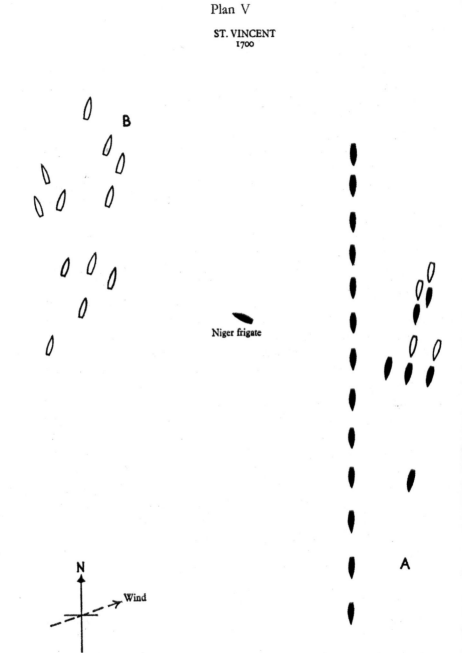

Niger frigate

B

N

Wind

A

A   *British fleet with prizes in tow*   B   *Spanish fleet in confusion to windward*
    'Captain' and 'Colossus' disabled

ships totally unfit for fight (*Concepcion, Mexicano, Solverano*), five unscathed, and from the rest he could not get any answer. At a council of war only three of his captains were in favour of renewing action. 'From the diversity of opinion, and considering the reply of each commander as an indication of the true state of his ship, I did not think it proper to force press of sail towards the enemy.' Instead, he withdrew to the southward, his flagship almost a wreck and an easy prey, should she be attacked. Jervis sent three frigates to look for her, but though they found her they never engaged. A week later the *Terpsichore* sighted her off the African coast and followed her for some days, but she could not herself engage such an enormous ship. Ultimately she reached Cadiz, where Cordova was arrested as soon as he landed and sent to Madrid under an escort of cavalry.

In his despatch, which was printed in the *Madrid Gazette* of March 10, he only mentions 6 officers killed and 342 men wounded, over 2000 prisoners in all having been taken. Duro, the Spanish naval historian of this *combate ignominioso* (as he calls it), lists 200 killed and 1284 wounded in the fleet as a whole, 200 casualties having been suffered on board the flagship alone. This figure is slightly higher than that given by English historians. Drinkwater puts the British casualties at 300 (73 killed and 227 wounded). This is an extremely light list, in view of the length of the action, but it must be remembered that captains were apt to exaggerate or minimise their lists of wounded, not killed, as they felt inclined. We know for certain that Jervis landed 2300 prisoners at Lagos two days later on parole that they would not serve against the British again until regularly exchanged. This condition was not honoured by Godoy (the so-called Prince of Peace, of whom Jervis wrote that 'since he has begun to scold I am doubtful of his sex') so that the Admiral exclaimed: 'The Lord have mercy on them, should they fall into my hands, for I will show them none.'

The British fleet lay to during the night of the 14th. They were some distance to leeward of the Spanish fleet, which they could see huddled together in great confusion. They themselves were in admirable order once more, a close-hauled, line-ahead formation lying between the enemy and the prizes, which were in tow of the frigates, as was also the *Captain*. Nelson had shifted his pennant to the *Irresistible* because, to quote the master's log in which his beloved ship is spoken of as if she was a living thing, 'our standing rigging and running rigging, with all the bending sails, was cut to pieces. Our wheel and fore topmast shot away, and the other masts severely wounded, the main mast having three shots through the heart.' The ship would not answer the helm and almost all her ammunition had been expended. Her crew was depleted, not only by heavy casualties, but by the fact that she had provided two prize crews and a fire party, since a fire had broken out in two places on board the *San Nicolas* after her capture. On account of all this, the *Minerve* frigate had to separate her from her prizes in order to take her in tow.

The next day Jervis awaited a renewal of the battle, for he was in no position to attack himself. Apart from the very considerable damage to rigging which all his ships had sustained, the expenditure of ammunition had been prodigious. Yet not a gun had burst, a rare feature in an eighteenth century battle. The *Prince George* expended 197 barrels of powder, the *Blenheim* 180, the *Culloden* 170 and the *Captain* 146. The day after, when Cordova's fleet drew away to the southward in the direction of Cadiz, Jervis anchored in Lagos Bay to land his prisoners and repair the damage to his fleet. There, on the morning of the 16th, he sent the following letter to all his captains:

> No language I am possessed of can convey the high sense I entertain of the exemplary conduct of the flag-officers, captains, officers, seamen, marines and soldiers, embarked on board every ship of the squadron I have honour to command, present at the vigorous and successful attack made upon the fleet of Spain on the 14th instant. The signal advantage obtained by His Majesty's arms on that day is entirely owing to their determined valour and discipline; and I request that you will accept yourself, and give my thanks and approbation to those composing the crew of the ship under your command.
>
> I am, Sir, your most humble servant,
> J. JERVIS.

5

Aftermath

ON THE EVENING after the battle Nelson rowed over to the *Victory* before he changed into a clean uniform. Part of his cocked hat had been shot away, his coat was torn in several places, and his face was still stained with sweat and powder. Jervis received him on the quarter-deck, clasped him in his arms (a most unusual gesture) and 'said he could not sufficiently thank me, and used every expression to make me happy'.

We can therefore imagine the asperity in the admiral's voice when, after Nelson left, Calder hinted that the commodore's manœuvre had been, to say the least, unauthorised. 'It certainly was so', snapped the old man, 'and if ever you commit such a breach of your orders I will forgive you also.'

Back on board the *Irresistible*, says Nelson, 'my bruises were looked at, and found to be trifling, and a few days made me as well as ever.' But this was not, in fact, the case. Although this was the only battle (apart from Copenhagen) in which the accident-prone little man did not suffer a serious injury, the bruises were actually an internal contusion which troubled him for the rest of his life. Indeed, the pain which it caused him at the time may be responsible for the briefest letter he ever wrote to his wife: 'I am well; Josiah is well.'

Hardly less perfunctory is the letter which followed two days later (on February 16, 1797): 'My dear Fanny,—I am most perfectly well and rich in honour, as is Josiah and Hoste. It would not be right to attempt detailing the action, as it will come from a much better pen than mine. God bless you and my dear father and believe me ever, your most affectionate husband, HORATIO NELSON.'

But if he did not have much to say to Fanny after the action, he

wrote a most generous note to Collingwood: 'My dearest friend,—
"A friend in need is a friend indeed" was never more truly verified
than by most noble and gallant conduct yesterday in sparing the
Captain from further loss; and I beg, both as a public officer and a
friend, you will accept my most sincere thanks. . . . We shall meet at
Lagos; but I could not come near you without assuring you how
sensible I am of your assistance in nearly a critical situation. Believe
me, as ever, your most affectionate, H.N.'

To which Collingwood replied the next morning: 'My dear good
friend,—First let me congratulate you on the success of yesterday,—
on the brilliancy it attached to the British Navy, and the humility it
must cause to its enemies,—and then let me congratulate my dear
Commodore on the distinguished part which he ever takes when the
honour and interests of his Country are at stake. It added very much
to the satisfaction which I felt in thumping the Spaniards that I
released you a little. The highest rewards are due to you and *Culloden*:
you formed the plan of attack, we were only accessories to the Don's
ruin; for, had they got on the other tack, they would have sooner
joined, and the business would have been less complete. . . . I am
ever, my dear friend, affectionately yours, COLLINGWOOD.'

The less attractive side of Nelson's character is, of course, his
vanity. Since this was the first occasion on which he was brought
into the public eye, he was determined that his exploit should lose
nothing in the telling. Elliot and Drinkwater would be the first home,
so it was important that they should be well primed. The morning
after the battle he went on board the *Lively* to see Sir Gilbert.
Finding that he had already gone over to the flagship, he said to
Drinkwater 'I hoped to have caught him before he saw the Admiral;
but come below with me.'

As they sat down in the cabin, Drinkwater offered his congratu-
lations which the commodore received 'with great modesty, though
evidently with great satisfaction'. The colonel then asked if there
were any details which might be added to the notes he had made of
the battle. Nelson needed no pressing. 'I'll tell you how it happened',
and he launched into the story of the Patent Bridge, 'a prompt and
extraordinary measure', as he called it, which checked the Spanish
fleet, though he confessed that his principal reason for boarding the
San Nicolas was to prevent her surrendering to the *Culloden*.

All this Drinkwater wrote down in pencil as fast as Nelson could dictate. He then turned to the question of rewards and honours. '"The Admiral will of course be made a Peer, and his seconds in command noticed accordingly. As for you, Commodore, they will make you a Baronet." The word was scarcely uttered when placing his hand on my arm, and looking me most expressively in the face, he said, "No, no; if they want to mark my services, it must not be in that manner." "Oh", I said, "you wish to be made a Knight of the Bath?" "Yes," replied Nelson, "if my services have been of any value let them be noticed in a way that the public may know me, or them."'

As Nelson foresaw, Drinkwater's notes were passed to Sir Gilbert and by him to the First Lord as soon as they reached London on March 3. The Order of the Bath was conferred before the end of the month and Nelson (by order of seniority) was promoted Rear-Admiral of the Blue. For his coat of arms (reproduced as Fig. 12) he chose as supporters 'on one side a Sailor, properly habited, holding in his hand the Broad Pendant on a staff and trampling a Spanish flag; on the other side, the British Lion. Crest—on a wreath of colours, the stern of a Spanish man-of-war, inscribed *San Josef.* Motto— Faith and Works.'

In addition to the narrative previously referred to, which Nelson wrote for the Duke of Clarence, he sent home a light-hearted skit which he called 'Commodore Nelson's Receipt for an Olla Podrida'. A few sentences will illustrate the humour of 'Nelson's New Art of Cookery'.

> Take a Spanish First Rate and an 80-gun Ship, and after well battering and basting for an hour, keep throwing in your force balls, and be sure to let them be well seasoned.
> Your fire must never slacken for a single moment, but must be kept up as brisk as possible during the whole time. . . .
> Your Olla Podrida may now be considered as completely dished, fit to set before His Majesty.

Fanny Nelson's reply to all this high-spirited jubilation gives a hint of the coolness which was to wreck the marriage: 'What can I say to you about Boarding? You have been wonderfully Protected; you have done desperate actions enough. Now may I—indeed I do— beg that you never Board again! LEAVE IT FOR CAPTAINS.'

In this connection it is worth noting that Nelson had already met Lady Hamilton socially, and had already corresponded with Sir William at Naples. When he took off the Governor from Elba he notified Sir William, adding 'with my most sincere regards, respects I ought to say, to Lady Hamilton and you'. The action between the *Minerve* and *Sabina* was described in detail for her benefit, and he was prompt to inform her that he had been promoted Rear-Admiral and invested with the Order of the Bath after the battle of St. Vincent.

The commander-in-chief was raised to the peerage with the title of Baron Jervis of Meaford in the County of Stafford and (at the King's suggestion) Earl of St. Vincent. He was also granted a pension of £3000 a year. The elevation to an earldom was unusual, but is explained by the fact that Jervis had been informed a fortnight before the battle that the King intended to raise him to the peerage, so that he was in fact a baron before the battle was fought. In 1801 he was created a viscount. Vice-Admirals Thompson and Parker became baronets and since Waldegrave already possessed a title he was given an Irish peerage. Calder was knighted, as was customary for those whose position in the fleet entitled them to bring home a despatch of victory.

It was this despatch which cast the only shadow on the jubilant aftermath of the first British victory for three years. A commander-in-chief is always in the invidious position of having to decide whose names are to be mentioned. After Howe's victory the worst course was taken of mentioning some but not others, and we have seen how Collingwood reacted to the omission of his name, 'a slight which nearly broke my heart', as he told his wife. The long-standing grievance was now avenged: 'I cannot help feeling an almost spiteful satisfaction that Lord Howe is outdone. His First of June, grand as it was, bears no proportion, in any respect, to this. There, the number of ships was nearly equal; here, the enemy was nearly double—28 guns more would have made them double our force.' Even then, when a gold medal was awarded to every captain who took part in the battle, he told the admiral that he could not accept his as long as his First of June medal was withheld: 'I feel that I was then improperly passed over; and to receive such distinction now would be to acknowledge the propriety of that injustice.' Not until

13 *'Captain'
engaging 'San
Nicolas'*

14 *'Salvador del
Mundo' in tow of
'Namur'*

15 *'Captain' in
tow of 'Minerve'*

Vignettes from Dalrymple's 'Narrative of the Battle of St. Vincent'

the First Lord had sent him a personal letter and medals for both actions was his proud spirit mollified.

Jervis's despatch, dated Lagos Bay, February 16, is printed in the Appendix of this volume. It mentions no names, save that of Calder. The account of the action is so bare and impersonal that it caused a murmuring in the fleet and a general demand for a more detailed narrative: hence Drinkwater's anonymous publication, which, however, did not receive wide circulation outside the service.

But in fact Jervis had written two despatches. The first was suppressed at Calder's instigation when he reminded the admiral of the fate of Howe's despatch and 'the inconvenience that has been found to result on other occasions from the practice of naming officers'. He even had the effrontery (according to Barrow, who later became Secretary of the Admiralty) to suggest that 'as Nelson had disobeyed the signal of recall, any eulogy of his conduct would encourage other officers to do the same'. The first draft was therefore replaced by the despatch we now have, though this was accompanied by a long personal letter to the First Lord in which Jervis wrote: 'The correct conduct of every officer and man in the squadron on the 14th inst, made it improper to distinguish one more than another in my public letter; yet to your Lordship it becomes me to state that Captain Troubridge in the *Culloden* led the squadron through the enemy in a masterly style, and was gallantly supported by the *Blenheim, Prince George, Orion, Irresistible* and *Colossus*. . . . Commodore Nelson contributed very much to the fortune of the day, as did Captain Collingwood.' For Hallowell, 'whose conduct on board the *Victory* during the action has made him more dear to me than before,' he begged the command of a large frigate, since he was temporarily without a ship. He added a word of praise for Admiral Parker and concluded: 'for the rest I beg to refer you to Captain Calder, who is thoroughly master of the subject'.

The modest and taciturn old man was clearly satisfied, even if no one else was, with his published despatch. As he told a friend the same day: 'I wish most heartily the public would be satisfied with accounts of actions in the style of Sir George Wootton, for although I do not profess to like fighting, I would much rather have an action with the enemy than detail one.' Wootton's style, it should be explained, was simply to state that he had taken, burned or destroyed 'of the enemy, as per margin'.

Nelson's character was the opposite. He was always his best public relations officer, and the publication of his own account did him no good among tight-lipped colleagues. One can only guess what St. Vincent himself thought of it, but we do know that Admiral Parker took umbrage at what he regarded as a slight on the ships composing his own division. Certainly the logs of the ships do not support Nelson's statement that the *Captain* and *Culloden* remained for any length of time unsupported, and there is no doubt that ships like Parker's *Prince George*, *Orion* and *Blenheim* bore their full share of the burden of the day. So, when Nelson's narrative appeared in print, Parker sent him a letter which concludes with words not normally printed in Nelsonian biographies:

> I am well aware that people in action know but little of occurrences in their rear, yet when a letter is written to be exposed to public view, positive assertions should be made with circumspection. I observed nothing but gallantry and good conduct in every ship that came under my observation, from first to last, and think myself equally entitled to an acknowledgement of a proportion of the success of that day with any man present at it. I feel much concern at the occasion of this letter, but remain etc. PARKER.

From this it is clear that Collingwood's comment in a private letter written immediately after the battle was not justified in the end, because this battle (like so many others) was fought all over again by participants equally jealous of honour and good fame. 'What is particularly happy in this great event', wrote Collingwood, 'is that there is no drawback, no slander. Though all were not equally engaged, I understand the Admiral has wisely avoided all partial praise of particular acts which might insinuate to the disadvantage of those whose hard luck prevented their getting into conspicuous situations.'

On February 24 Jervis took his fleet back to Lisbon, which for the next two years was to be his base in watching any threat on the part of the Spanish at Cadiz. He had defeated the first stage of the grand design to invade the British Isles by a combination of the fleets of France and Spain. The Mediterranean lay open once more to British shipping and as soon as Pitt's diplomacy could reconstruct another alliance of the central powers, Nelson would be detached to fight the campaign which culminated in the battle of the Nile the next year.

Though as Sir John Jervis or as Earl of St. Vincent the old admiral never enjoyed the nation-wide popularity which was won by his subordinate, he had the satisfaction of knowing that the fleets which he trained were now capable of being led to victory by one who enjoyed public applause. He himself detested 'parade'. The sort of gratitude he appreciated was that shown by the young Captain Mark Kerr when, on the return of the fleet to Lisbon, Jervis recalled a promise to give him a command. Summoning him to the cabin of the *Victory*, he led him to the stern window to see the prizes lying in the Tagus. 'Mark', he said, 'I promised you a post commission if I fell in with the enemy at daylight, or in a fog. I did both. There it is', and he put a captain's commission into the young man's hand, 'and that is the ship'—pointing to the *San Ysidro*. 'You are to go on board directly and bring her to a safe anchorage.'

6

The Mutinies

BETWEEN THE BATTLE of St. Vincent in February and the battle
of Camperdown in October Britain passed through the gravest
crisis in the history of her navy. This was due to the mutiny of the
Channel fleet at Spithead in April, whence the trouble spread to the
Nore command during the summer and thence to Admiral Duncan's
ships at Yarmouth, as well as to Plymouth and elsewhere. Only the
Mediterranean fleet escaped the mischief, owing to the prompt
measures taken by Lord St. Vincent against ships which might have
brought the infection from England; for the loyalty of his own ships
he had no fear, because morale was high on account of the recent
victory.

It was not so much the actual events of the mutiny which en-
dangered the safety of the country, as their timing during that year
of invasion threats. As Melville wrote in *Billy Budd* (the only work of
genius which those events produced): 'To the British Empire the
Nore mutiny was what a strike in the fire brigade would be to London
threatened by general arson.' It was indeed really a strike to obtain
scandalously overdue improvements in service conditions. Looking
back on the shameful overcrowding, the barbarous and filthy
circumstances in which seamen lived at that date, it is difficult not
to sympathise with the mutineers at the start.

There had been grumblings of discontent throughout the winter.
Specific grievances were first listed in illiterate petitions which
began to reach Lord Howe at Bath at the very time of the victory
off Cape St. Vincent. But Howe was only nominally in command of
the Channel fleet: the sluggish Lord Bridport was in effective
command. These petitions, now preserved in the Public Record
Office, are cast in very similar language, though written in a variety

of almost illiterate hands. They suggest a common source of origin which has never been identified, beyond the fact that a quartermaster's mate in the flagship named Valentine Joyce, aged twenty-six, and an ex-lawyer named Evans soon declared themselves the leaders of the 'delegates' which forbade the Channel fleet to put to sea on April 16.

When the news leaked out, says the *Annual Register*, the event appeared to the country 'so seemingly unnatural, and even supposed to be so remote from possibility, that it is difficult to say whether surprise, grief or terror was the predominant feeling which existed'.

It would not have been so surprising had the people of England realised the conditions under which the seamen lived, or had Lord Howe or Lord Spencer at the Admiralty acted with any wisdom or promptitude. Howe did nothing but forward the petitions to the Admiralty, because he thought their anonymity did not permit an answer. The Admiralty did nothing, because it was felt that the principal objective of the mutineers—an increase in pay, or at least an attempt to pay the men what was actually due to them—would, as Spencer wrote, 'make an enormous increase to our disbursements already sufficiently burthensome'.

The pay of an ordinary seaman was 19s. a month, a figure settled in Cromwell's day and unchanged ever since—surely the longest pay-pause in history. In fact it was less than the nominal sum, because 'sixpences' and 'groats' were always being deducted from the miserable total—sixpence to Greenwich Hospital, a groat to the chaplain on board, deductions for slop clothing, or total stoppage of pay if a man went sick. Even when a ship was paid off, often after several years' service at sea, the cash or wage ticket which remained would be exchanged for much below its nominal value with the Jews, bumboat women and prostitutes who infested the ports. Within a few days of glorious drunkenness in the taverns or brothels of Portsmouth, Plymouth or Sheerness, the seaman would be as penniless as he had been on board and easy game for the next press gang. As far as the officers of the Royal Navy were concerned, the profession offered prestige, pay and prize money adequate to their deserts. As far as seamen were concerned, it offered danger, hardship disease and poverty. If a sailor was serving in the Merchant Navy, as many of them did between enforced spells on board men-of-war, he could earn four or five times as much as in the Royal Navy, particularly in time of war. Even if he was fortunate enough to end his days 'safe moored in Greenwich tier', his pension in that hospital was half what it was in the military hospital at Chelsea.

Another grievance of which the seamen complained was, 'that our provisions be raised to the weight of 16 oz. to the pound, and of a better quality'. What they were aiming at was the iniquitous practice of pursers (at that date civilian officers) in selling short weights in order to recoup themselves for loss due to wastage of victuals. In any case, though the printed scale of food was generous enough, the quality was often so bad that most of it was uneatable—weevilly biscuits, sour beer and salt beef or pork so hard that it could not be masticated. The only issue which was appreciated was grog, and the commonest offence in the punishment books was that of drunkenness.

Other grievances have a bearing on the health of the Navy. 'That your lordships will be pleased seriously to look into the state of the sick on board H.M. ships, that they may be better attended to, and that they may have the use of such necessaries as are allowed to them in time of sickness; and that these necessaries be not embezzled.' Also, that if a man be wounded in action, it was requested that his pay might be continued until he was discharged cured. That surgeons embezzled the luxuries reserved for the sick has never been really established, but there is no doubt that at this stage of the war medical standards in the fleet were very low. A naval surgeon, as in Smollett's day, was still regarded as the lowest type in the profession. There were great men among them—Blane, Trotter and Baird, for example—but there was also a number of incompetent drunkards and raw apprentices from the Scottish medical schools. One great curse of the sea, the incidence of scurvy, was on the point of being removed owing to the efforts of Blane and Trotter to persuade the Admiralty to issue lemon juice regularly. This itself would not have been so necessary had the victualling authorities paid any attention to the pathetically innocent request of the mutineers that they 'should be granted sufficient quantity of vegetables of such kind as may be most plentiful in the ports to which we go; which we grievously complain and lay under the want of'.

To the modern reader, the most curious omission from their list of grievances is any mention of the barbarous punishments under which the men suffered daily. It is true that it was a more brutal age than ours and that the penal law of the land was even more savage than the Articles of War, which was the code they lived under. It is also true that by the regulations a captain could not order a flogging of more than twelve strokes with the cat-o'-nine-tails without a court martial. But it was the unofficial punishments, the constant 'startings' with a rope's end wielded by a tyrannical bosun's mate, which probably caused more damage to a man's health and certainly made life more of a hell than the formal 'seizing up' at the gratings, when the whole crew was turned up to witness punishment. Of course, it is impossible to generalise about this matter in the Navy as a whole, because while some ships were 'hells afloat', others were happy ships commanded by humane officers. Nevertheless, there were plenty of drunken sadists among the inferior officers at that date: captains of the calibre of St. Vincent's officers were rarer in Lord Bridport's fleet.

It was, in fact, lack of leadership and of a satisfactory officer–man relationship which was the basic cause of the mutinies. The divisional system was still in its infancy. We have seen the inglorious part played by the Channel fleet in the Bantry Bay affair, and such, broadly speaking had been the case for the past three years. What was needed was some striking victory, such as Cape St. Vincent, or those which Duncan and Nelson were to provide during the next decade, to raise the morale of men who hated the service and were, to say the least, bored by futile cruises to Brest and back. Month in and month out, what the men had to endure was discomfort, disease, tyranny and hunger. Even when they returned to port, shore leave was denied them on account of the danger of desertion. What could be more pathetic than their fourth demand: 'That we may be looked upon as a number of men standing in defence of our country; and that we may in somewise have grant and opportunity to taste the sweets of liberty on shore, when in any harbour, and when we have completed the duty of our ship, after our return from the sea.'

At no date was a high standard of leadership on the part of officers more necessary than in the year 1797. Two years previously, on account of the unpopularity of the King's service, and because a war fought on this scale made unprecedented demands on the manpower of the nation, Pitt had passed the Quota Acts, whereby every county and borough was scheduled to produce a certain number of men for the Navy. As long as ships were manned by professional seamen from the great ports, who had entered as boys, even as long as volunteers attracted by the generous bounties offered in wartime presented themselves at the rendezvous, the activities of the press gangs were limited. But when the scum of the waterfronts were rounded up by the impressment service, and above all when landmen, totally ignorant of the sea, were conscripted into the service, there was bound to be trouble. Dr. Johnson used to complain that 'a ship is worse than a gaol, because of the additional danger of drowning'; but by the time of Nelson ships were largely manned from the gaols. When magistrates found their quota was still short of men, they scoured the gaols for petty criminals who could be sent to sea. This brought on board an element of vice and disease of which ships in peace-time were innocent.

It was supposed by many officers at the time, and it has been frequently suggested since, that this was not a mutiny but a revolution, that, as one officer wrote, 'the character of the present mutiny is perfectly French'. But there is no trace of Jacobinism in all the records of those dangerous months. The Corresponding Societies may well have liked to contact the mutineers, but they seldom, if ever, succeeded in doing so. The men themselves strongly denied any political motives. 'We are not actuated by any spirit of sedition or disaffection, whatsoever,' the delegates told Charles James Fox; 'on the contrary, it is indigence and extreme penury alone that is the cause of our complaint.' We can well believe them, with the possible exception of the ten per cent of the fleet who were Irish, and therefore at this date sympathised with the unrest in Ireland caused by the United Irishmen party. Such men would never have been at sea, had it not been for the Quota Acts.

Collingwood's diagnosis in a letter written to his sister, which has recently been printed, represents the officer's point of view:

> The chief promoters in all this business have been what they call Billy Pitt's men—the county volunteers, your ruined politicians, who having drunk ale enough to drown a nation, and talked nonsense enough to mad it—your Constituent and Corresponding Society men, finding politics and faction too rare a diet to fat upon, took the county bounty and embarked with their budget of politics, and the education

of a Sunday school, into ships where they disseminated their nonsense and their mischief. These are the fellows who have done the business; the seamen who suffer are only the cat's paw. Making seamen's letters free of postage has very much promoted the business: every lazy fellow finds an excuse from work by writing a letter, and what kind of correspondence can you expect from the refuse of the gallows and the purging of the gaols, and such make a majority in most ships' companies in such a war as this.

Even if Collingwood exaggerates the number of sea-lawyers and the amount of frothy talk about liberty and equality which there was in the air at the time, the Quota Acts did more practical damage by introducing disease on board. Apart from scurvy, which was due to an easily avoidable vegetable deficiency, the commonest of the sea diseases was typhus—ship or gaol fever, as it was then called,— a louse-borne disease associated, as we have said, with ragged clothes and dirty living conditions. There are numerous instances of a man suffering from typhus coming straight out of gaol on to an overcrowded pressing tender, from which he was taken off without any change of clothes or form of washing to a man-of-war, whose ship's company he infected within a few days.

The following is the report of Surgeon John Snipe on the state of the *Sandwich*, the flagship at the Nore, which was the receiving ship for pressing tenders passing down the Thames. It is dated March 22 (four days after the original outbreak of mutiny at Spithead) and it is addressed to the captain of the ship who, on forwarding it to the Admiralty, wrote a covering letter in which he added that 'the Surgeon's statement is, I am sorry to say, a true picture of our situation'. Snipe was later Nelson's surgeon in the Mediterranean during the years preceding Trafalgar, when the standard of health was very different. By 'infection' and 'contagious fever' he means typhus, though the source of the disease and its cure was at that time totally unknown to the medical profession:

> Sir,—The infection which has existed for some time in H.M. ship *Sandwich* under your command having of late become more virulent and resisted the methods that have been taken to check it, which is solely owing to the ship being so crowded, I beg leave to acquaint you that it is absolutely necessary to reduce the numbers of men already on board. Those men that are first seized with the contagious

fever which has so alarmingly shown itself, are in general very dirty, almost naked, and in general without beds (having either lost them by their own indolence, or the villainy of their companions). . . .

I feel myself called upon to point out the little avail of prescribing medicines to unhappy sufferers, who are so bare of common necessaries and compelled to mix with the throng by laying on the decks. The numbers of sores, scalds and other unavoidable accidents, which the awkward landmen are liable to, often degenerate into bad ulcers, which cannot readily be cured on board, owing sometimes to their own bad habits, but oftener to the foul air they breathe between decks; besides being frequently trodden upon in the night from their crowded state.

Sir, it is my professional opinion, that there is no effective remedy, but by considerably reducing the number that have been usually kept for months in the *Sandwich*, for sickness and contagion cannot be prevented by any physical means where fifteen or sixteen hundred men are confined in the small compass of a ship, many of whom are vitiated in their habits, as well as filthy in their dispositions. The circumambient air is so impregnated with human effluvia that contagious fevers must inevitably be the consequence.

Such was the ship to which Richard Parker found himself drafted as a pressed man, having on two previous occasions served briefly in the Navy. On the first of these he was discharged for neurotic symptoms and on the second for insolence towards his commanding officer. He had recently been in a debtor's prison and is said to have been a village schoolmaster. Is it surprising that, faced with the sort of conditions he found on board, and favoured with some sort of education and certainly with the gift of the gab, he became the leader of a mutiny in sympathy with what was going on at Portsmouth, and whose natural vanity allowed himself to be pushed into the position of President of the Floating Republic, as he called it?

The seamen's petitions to Howe, and the subsequent repetition of their demands by the delegates representing the mutineers both at Spithead and the Nore, express the grievances uppermost in their minds. A good many officers who sympathised with them would have added more about the need to reform the methods of maintaining discipline, which, as we have seen, the men omitted. An interesting letter by Lieutenant Burney to the First Lord, which has recently come to light, illustrates a view which was common among humane and intelligent officers.

In spite of his comparatively junior rank, Burney's name must have been familiar to Spencer before he dared to write to him at the height of the troubles. He was the son of the well-known musician and man about town, Dr. Burney, the brother of the best-selling novelist Fanny Burney, and one of Cook's most reliable officers on the voyage round the world. In Burney's view, justice demanded a more equitable distribution of prize money (under existing regulations a seaman might get one guinea when a captain got a thousand), more liberty on shore, and a closer check on unofficial punishments. 'The misapplication of the Articles of War and the power of punishment vested in individual hands is too well known to require proof. I served in a ship where every one of the maintopmen were stripped and flogged at the gangway for no other cause than that another ship in company got her topgallant yards up first, and not for any wilful negligence on the part of our men. Had we been first, possibly the topmen of the other ship might have been the sufferers.'

There may also be something in Burney's explanation why the mutiny spread to Duncan's North Sea fleet—that the men suffered greater hardship serving on that station than on any other. When we learn that the pay, scandalously low as it was, was grossly in arrears on board many of those ships, and when we recall the effects of a hard winter's close blockade of the Dutch coast, we cannot be surprised at what Burney politely calls 'a degree of impatience' producing a mutiny.

Typical of the lack of understanding shown in this dangerous situation was the fact that neither Howe nor Spencer ever mentioned to Bridport that petitions had been dribbling in over the past few months. It was not until April 13, on the very eve of the outbreak, that Bridport happened to hear from one of his junior officers that representations to the Admiralty had been made by the crews under his command for an increase in pay. 'If this should be the case', the aggrieved commander-in-chief wrote to Spencer, 'it would be very desirable for me to know what steps have been taken in consequence thereof.'

Spencer's answer was, none. To put Bridport in the picture he did send him a selection of the petitions, but at the same date (April

16, Easter Sunday) he was given orders to put to sea. When these orders were transmitted to the captains of each ship, the crew of Howe's old flagship, *Queen Charlotte*, gave the signal for mutiny with an unauthorised burst of cheering. This was taken up throughout the fleet and not a ship moved from her moorings. With the efficiency which was to characterise all the events at Spithead, a party of seamen from the *Queen Charlotte* immediately toured the fleet in boats to summon two delegates from each ship to meet that evening. The mutiny had begun.

The unfortunate Bridport could now only tell his captains to muster their ship's companies in order to find out what was wrong. Urgent messages were also sent to London to bring the First Lord to the scene, but by the time Spencer arrived on the 18th the delegates had organised themselves, issued regulations and taken charge of the fleet.

All that the First Lord had to offer was an increase of 3s. a month in the pay of ordinary seamen: the other complaints were contemptuously ignored. Naturally the delegates unanimously refused the offer, but at the same time they stated that no additional demands would be made: 'We know when to cease to ask, as well as to begin; we ask nothing but what is moderate, and may be granted without detriment to the nation or injury to the service.'

Even then Spencer refused further negotiations. The senior officers, still by sufferance on board their ships, were told to read out to the men a second reply which went no further than the first. The mutineers refused to consider it until a Royal Pardon had been issued. At this Spencer admitted defeat and rode off through the night to Windsor, but only to obtain the pardon, not to redress the grievances.

An uneasy pause followed his departure. To Lieutenant Beaver on board H.M.S. *Monarch* it seemed that 'Lord Spencer and the other Lords of the Admiralty trifle too much. . . . The seamen still continue to conduct themselves incredibly well, performing the usual duties with alacrity, and behaving towards their officers with the greatest respect. I had always great respect for an English seaman; I like the character now better than ever.' The men had even rowed a visiting German prince round the fleet and given him the salutes befitting his rank.

As soon as the King's Pardon was printed and copies had been rushed down to Portsmouth, the Admiralty imagined that all was over. But when the delegates examined the official answer to their complaints they were as disgusted as ever. It was flatly stated that any increase in the distribution of flour in port was out of the question. As for vegetables, 'instead of asking for more, they ought to be most thankful for that which, at great expense to the country, they are now supplied'.

On the last day of April news arrived that the ships at Plymouth had mutinied and the first grumblings of discontent were heard from Duncan's ships at Yarmouth. The leaders at Spithead therefore decided that until their grievances were met by an Act of Parliament they would not shift from the position they had taken up.

Another effort was made to get the fleet to sail on May 7, but again the crews refused to obey orders, this time to the accompaniment of shouts of 'an Act of Parliament and an honest three pounds of pork'. As they had done for the preceding fortnight, boats toured the fleet to give the crews the party line. On this occasion Admiral Sir John Colpoys, whose behaviour during the Bantry Bay affair had not endeared him to his men, refused to allow the delegates to come on board his ship. A party of seamen on the fo'c'sle thereupon unleashed a gun and pointed it at the quarter-deck. The first lieutenant warned them that he would fire if they did not desist. One of the men dared him to do so. He fired and the man fell dead.

Immediately the whole crew forced their way forward shouting, 'Blood for blood!' There was a good deal of wild shooting, in which three men were killed and several others, including a delegate, were wounded. A rope was rove to haul the first lieutenant up to the yard-arm, but Valentine Joyce, the leading spirit of the whole affair, thrust his way forward to stop further bloodshed and at the same time Colpoys bravely shouted that the responsibility was his. 'You're a damned bloody scoundrel', shrieked one of the 800 men now facing him. 'How dare you speak to the admiral in that manner?' shouted another. Tension relaxed while the ship's surgeon persuaded the men to give Colpoys a hearing.

This was the only truly violent episode in the whole mutiny. But the delegates had not yet gained their point. Colpoys's speech did not satisfy them, so he and other officers were put under arrest before being formally tried and found guilty of murder. Unpopular officers of other ships were hustled ashore and more blood would certainly have been shed—particularly that of Colpoys—had not the news arrived that a Seamen's Bill had been rushed through Parliament in record time and had received the Royal Assent, in addition to the Royal Pardon.

On May 10 'Black Dick' Howe, the sailor's friend and still the nominal commander of the fleet, was told by the Admiralty to carry the news to every ship at Spithead by rowing round the fleet in a boat manned by the delegates. The exertions made by the seventy-one-year old admiral during the next three days nearly killed him, but they do atone for his extraordinary blindness to the seriousness of the situation in its early stages. He climbed up over the side of one ship after another to read the news and wave the pardon in the faces of the men, many of whom could not read. At the end of it all he asked Joyce and other delegates to meet him at the governor's house on shore. There, in a typically naval way, everything was settled over a glass of wine, followed by a grand procession through the town.

The dignified manner in which Bridport accepted the way the Admiralty took the matter out of his control by playing the trump card of Howe's popularity with the sailors does much to commend him. But nothing can excuse the inept handling of the whole affair by their Lordships, and by Spencer in particular. In an inflammable situation they nearly started the whole trouble again by demanding that the fleet should sail on the first tide. Fortunately the wind did not serve until May 17, when the Channel fleet, with the Union Jack instead of the Red Flag of the Mutineers at the masthead of every ship, put to sea to resume the blockade of Brest exactly a month after the beginning of the mutiny.

For the Navy, however, the troubles were not yet over, because a much more serious situation developed at the Nore and at Yarmouth, even though the passing of the Seamen's Act had recognised the justice of the demands made by the men at Spithead.

On May 12 a self-appointed committee of delegates met on board the *Sandwich* at the Nore. From the description we have given of conditions prevailing on board this ship, the fact is not surprising; nor, from what we know of Richard Parker's gifts as a demagogue, is the fact that he soon found himself in the position of leader. But what was he to do when, soon after the first irrevocable step had been taken to mutiny, a frigate arrived from Spithead with the news that all was over and her crew had returned to duty? Parker's reaction was the first of many forcible conversions to his cause among the ships at the Nore. One of the line-of-battle ships which happened to be in the river was sent alongside the frigate with her gun ports open, ready to fire a broadside. The consequence was that the frigate's crew rapidly reconsidered their position, though they managed to escape from Parker's threat a few days later.

This was the first instance of the rougher attitude which the Nore mutineers were to adopt. Parker was adept at persuading and bullying those who had not made up their minds and at working up a hysterical atmosphere by constant speechifying, with boats continually going to and fro between the ships as they swung at their buoys, playing popular tunes—notably, with supreme ineptness, *Rule Britannia.*

He had to think up some fresh demands to present to Admiral Buckner, a singularly colourless man. At that date the Nore was a separate command from Duncan's North Sea fleet based on Yarmouth. But since Sheerness was the only large victualling base, Duncan's ships were constantly entering or leaving the river Thames. The only permanent force under Buckner's command was the receiving ship *Sandwich* and three old guard ships which never left their moorings. Other ships were but temporary visitors and Buckner was really only a port admiral.

Parker's demands, signed by him as 'President' of the Floating Republic, were presented on May 20, three days after the Channel fleet had put to sea. In the first place he asked that 'every indulgence granted to the fleet at Portsmouth be granted to His Majesty's subjects serving in the fleet at the Nore'. The Seamen's Act had already covered this point. His other demands were all concerned with more regular pay, a juster distribution of prize money and a revision of the Articles of War—much as Burney suggested in his letter.

The demands were moderate enough, just as the earlier ones had been, but once more the Admiralty instructed Buckner to refuse the lot. Once more Spencer was humiliated by having to go down to

Sheerness, where the inn at which he stayed was besieged by riotous and insolent sailors who compelled him to return to London to reconsider his attitude.

It was obvious that a far more dangerous situation was now facing the country. Parker's delegates were treating their officers much more brusquely than had been the case at Portsmouth. He boldly announced his intention to blockade the port of London by refusing to allow any vessels to pass up or down the river.

Sterner measures were therefore adopted by the authorities. The garrison at Sheerness was rapidly reinforced. The victualling yard was instructed to withhold supplies of food and water from the ships in the river and the Secretary of the Admiralty asked Duncan if he could use the North Sea fleet based on Yarmouth against the dissident ships in the Thames. Even more sinister was the despatch of the famous Captain Bligh (who had been turned out of his ship at the Nore) to Yarmouth in order to consult with Duncan.

The Admiral's reply was as follows:

> My dear Sir,—Your two letters of the 21st and 22nd was yesterday secured. The last requires some delicacy to answer. The fleet here continues to behave well, and I am sure will refuse no common service. At the same time, to call them who have kept in order to chastise those at the Nore, in my opinion would subject them to a disagreeable jealousy from all other parts of the fleet who engaged in this unhappy business; but for all this I don't shrink from the business if it cannot otherwise be got the better of; and this day having occasion to speak to my ship's company, a thing I have lately practised much, from what happened last night I touched gently on what I might expect from them in support of my flag and self in the execution of my duty. They to a man said they were ready and willing at all times to obey my commands.

He was a good deal too optimistic. When the news of the original outbreak reached his ships, which were based on Yarmouth for the purpose of blockading the Dutch fleet in the Texel, he told the First Lord that, 'I will answer for it, there will be no more of it in the North Sea fleet'. But even when he wrote there were signs of discontent on board his own flagship, the *Venerable*. On April 30 the men swarmed into the fore-shrouds and gave three unauthorised cheers. Their gigantic admiral (Adam Duncan was six feet four inches

16 *A Flogging: George Cruikshank's*
illustration to a story entitled 'The Point
of Honour', by G. Barker

17 *Captain William*
Bligh

From an engraving by J.
Condy after J. Russell

18 *The Delegates in Council*
From a coloured etching by I. *Cruikshank*

19 *Death mask of Richard Parker*

tall), bursting with indignation, had to be restrained by the chaplain from running a ringleader through with his sword. However, unlike Bridport and Buckner, Duncan was a natural leader of men, respected and beloved by those who came into direct contact with him. He was also a much more determined man. He was certainly not going to haul down his flag for the asking. Mastering his fury, he asked the men what they wanted and promised to make representations to have their grievances redressed in respect of the scandalous arrears of pay which existed in so many ships. He had himself previously recommended that the number of lashes in a flogging should be reduced. He was one of the first to request that lemon juice should be distributed to combat scurvy, and his whole record suggests that he was really on the side of the men. But he was not going to permit mutinous behaviour in any ship under his command. His address to his own ship's company a week later gives us the measure of the man: he was always an awkward speaker, but his sincerity rings through his halting words.

My Lads,—Fearing some part I intend to say to you might escape me, I have written it down.

You have had a week to reflect on what happened on Sunday last, and, I doubt not, will agree with me in thinking your conduct was highly improper. I know many of you think so.

The reddress most graciously given by His Majesty, who you all know is the best of Kings, to the requests of the fleet at Spithead, was read to you, and you seemed pleased with it.

The bad example from this ship brought others into the same situation, and ended, as in this ship, without its being known what was wanted or intended. I will venture to say you was misled by a few designing men, and those not the best characters, some of whom I know and saw active. I would advise them to guard their conduct well, as I shall keep a strict eye on them; nor can they expect to be longer petty officers in this ship. Others I also know who shrank from the business, and behaved as they ought. They shall always have a claim in my favour. I hear it rumoured, though I give no credit to it, that the ship's company will refuse to go to sea. As a matter of that kind should not be doubtful, I ask you, and I shall ask every ship in the fleet, is that your determination?

The reply he received was as follows:

Most worthy and honoured sir, Not having the gift of speech of accosting you in a proper manner, we the ship's company of H.M. ship *Venerable* having taken into consideration the weighty affair which was so indiscreetly committed on the 30th ult. and for which we are sincerely ashamed of we theirfore think it our duty to return you our most sincere and hearty thanks for so graciously forgiving us the rash step which we took on that fatal day and so we humbly implore your honour's pardon with hearts full of gratitude and tears in our eyes for the offence we have given to the wortheyest of commanders who as [*sic*] proved a father to us and as such we shall allways honour you. . . .

Nevertheless, on May 13 there was another outbreak of cheering, this time on board the *Adamant*. Duncan had himself rowed across to the ship and made one of his brief speeches to the crew. He concluded by asking if anyone present contested his authority. One of his audience replied insolently 'I do!' Thereupon the admiral seized him by the collar and held him over the side of the ship with one arm, exclaiming: 'My lads, look at this fellow, he who dares to deprive me of the command of the fleet!' The consequence was that when he put their obedience to the test by ordering the fleet to sea, the *Venerable* and the *Adamant* followed him; but the crews of other ships which had not come under his personal influence refused.

Part of the trouble was that the Nore ships were now trying to persuade those at Yarmouth to follow their example. Already one of Duncan's best ships, the *Director*, which had been sent to the Nore to refit, had mutinied. The captain of this ship was none other than William Bligh, the victim of the notorious *Bounty* mutiny eight years previously. It is the fashion nowadays to whitewash Bligh, because of his skill as a navigator and his undoubted courage. But the extraordinary sequence of mutinies and quarrels which marred his career—whether as captain of the *Bounty*, or of the *Director*, or as Governor of New South Wales—cannot be purely coincidental. There seems to have been something arrogant about the man which alienated feelings of loyalty, not only among his men but among his officers.

However, in the case of the Mutiny at the Nore, we must not traduce Bligh. It is sometimes said that he was the first captain to be sent on shore by the mutineers, but this is to confuse him with his namesake, John Bligh, captain of the *Latona*. In the *Director*, all the officers were retained on board with the exception of the captain, who described the state of his ship to the Admiralty in the following terms: 'Hitherto, never did a ship's company behave better, or did ever a ship bear the marks of content and correctness.' Furthermore, when the mutiny was over and Bligh had returned on board, he intervened with the authorities on behalf of his men, reducing the number of those who were refused pardon from thirty-one to ten. Some of those who were transported to Botany Bay as a punishment met Bligh again when he became Governor of New South Wales. In return for his clemency in 1797, he extorted from his crew a promise of good behaviour in the future. This promise was honoured by all his men with a single exception, a man who was described as 'an old offender', who was court martialled in October for his continued efforts 'to excite mutiny and for disobeying the lawful commands of his officers when at sea'. The way the rest of the crew fought at the battle of Camperdown shows their gratitude.

Soon after mutiny had broken out on board the *Director*, the Nore delegates sent a cutter to invite the seamen at Yarmouth to join them. In the words of an anonymous ballad monger, Neptune demanded that they should join forces—

> '*Awake, my sons*', *the watery monarch said,*
> '*The torpid vapours from your souls remove;*
> *Inspire yourselves with true fraternal love.*
> *Unto the Nore repair without delay;*
> *There join your brothers with a loud Huzza.*'

The delegates were, however, intercepted by Duncan on May 23, and on the 26th he determined to put to sea. Four ships refused to sail and a few days later the rest returned to their anchorage, or followed their companions to the Nore on the excuse that their wages remained unpaid. Two only of the North Sea fleet of 13 ships accompanied the admiral to the mouth of the Texel—the flagship *Venerable* and the *Adamant*. There for three days Duncan blockaded the whole of the Dutch fleet by making signals to an imaginary fleet which was supposed to be lying below the horizon.

As he told his own ship's company in the bitterness of his heart: 'My lads, I once more call you together with a sorrowful heart from what I have lately seen—the disaffection of the fleet: I call it disaffection, for the crews have no grievances. To be deserted by my fleet in the face of the enemy is a disgrace which, I believe, never before happened to a British admiral, nor could I have supposed it possible. My greatest comfort, under God, is that I have been supported by the officers, seamen and marines of this ship; for which, with a heart overflowing with gratitude, I request you to accept my thanks. I flatter myself that much good may result from your example, by bringing those deluded people to a sense of duty which they owe, not only to their King and country, but to themselves. . . . It has often been my pride, with you, to look into the Texel and see a foe which dreaded coming out to meet us. My pride is humbled now. My feelings are not easily to be expressed. Our cup is overflowing and has made us wanton. The all-wise Providence has given us this check as a warning, and I hope we shall improve by it. On him then let us trust, where our only security can be found. I find there are many good men among you; I have had full confidence in all in this ship, and once more beg to express my approbation of your conduct. May God, who has this far conducted you, continue to do so; and may the British navy, the glory and support of our country, be restored to its wonted splendour, and be not only the bulwark of Britain, but the terror of the world. But this can only be effected by a strict adherence to our duty and obedience; and let us pray that Almighty God may keep us all in the right way of thinking. God bless you all!' We are told by an onlooker that this speech was delivered in such an impressive manner that there was not a dry eye among the admiral's audience.

Knowing as we do now the enemy side of the strategic picture at the moment, the mutiny of Duncan's fleet was the most dangerous of all. It was the ideal opportunity for an invasion from the Texel, instead of one from Brest. The details of such plans will be more fully considered in our next chapter. For the present, leaving Duncan on watch off the mouth of the Texel, we may turn to the incidents which occurred among his dissident ships as they made their way down from Yarmouth to the Nore.

From the letters of a young midshipman on board the *Nassau*, which have only recently come to light, we have a unique record of the sequence of events. Alexander Hardy is writing to his family in Ireland, then also in the throes of rebellion. The men on board his

64-gun ship had ample reason for joining the mutineers since, in the humblest terms, they had already pointed out to the authorities that they had nineteen months' wages owing to them and that most of them 'were in general want of almost every article of wearing apparel'.

On May 20 Hardy writes from Yarmouth Roads: 'I am sorry to say that we are in a bad state here as you are at home—Mutinies almost every day and I daily dread the consequences of them. We remained quiet for some time, but have broke out again. . . . Yarmouth is in an uproar: the seamen are committing great depredations, beating and evil treating all the inhabitants and breaking windows etc., so that no people venture out after dark. Our ship, I believe all the fleet is the same, in a state of intoxication from 2 to 8 o'clock.' On May 30 the *Nassau*, in company with other ships, ran for the Nore under the Red Flag, though, curiously enough, they hauled it down in order to celebrate the anniversary of the Restoration of Charles II.

Hardy's next letter is therefore from the Nore: 'My dear Father, I have but just time to tell that the people have broke out worse than ever, have hoisted the Bloody Flag and loaded the guns fore and aft, resolved to engage any ship that comes alongside. We have given up the command of the ship to them. I am sorry to say that all is anarchy and confusion on board the *Nassau*. The people have the entire command of her and only pay that respect to their officers they usually did when duty was going on; when last I wrote I mentioned my doubts of the people going to sea without their pay, which is now really the case.'

Off Sheerness on June 3 he continues: 'I have been very unhappy since this business has taken place and when they were bringing the ship up and hearing them cheer I could not hold out no longer but went to my cot and shed tears there for the space of two hours, thinking to what a pitch our men had got to in defiance of their King and Country, and since have passed my time in a state of stupid silence to everybody; the people turned one of the midshipmen on shore, but the remainder of us will sleep on board and all that I can do to provoke them to turn me on shore will not do, for I am told by them that I am too well liked and will be one of the last that they will turn out of the ship.

'On Wednesday evening I imagined that everything was coming to a crisis in our favour—but it was only a faint hope. The business was thus: our men came aft and one and all said they were ashamed of their conduct, begged the officers' pardon and hoped that they would get the King's pardon likewise, and were so sincere that most of them shed tears; I was for that time full of spirits in hopes of our ship's company plan succeeding. The next morning they went round the ships that came with us who only wanted their pay and told them they would have nothing to do with the *Sandwich* and when we got our pay to go to sea; but all objected to it, saying they will stick to the *Sandwich* until their grievances are redressed. Our men came back very much dejected and are against their will obliged to stay here with the Red Flag up, so that our hopes are blasted.'

At that date Parker and the delegates on board the *Sandwich* were still in control. Matters were approaching a civil war. While the Government moved more troops into Sheerness and sent down Lord Keith (the Captain Elphinstone of Bantry Bay) to take over from the incompetent Buckner, Parker and the mutinous ships blockaded the river Thames. Volunteers to serve against the mutineers were called for, and ships and crews of the East India Company were conscripted. The Younger Brothers of Trinity House were told to hold themselves in readiness for emergency service, and the Government proposed to starve the fleet into submission by prohibiting the despatch of victuals from Sheerness. Bundles of proclamations were stuffed into the pockets of the sick which had been sent on shore for medical treatment, but after these unfortunates had been sent back to their ships the following note was put on board the returning boat:

> For the Lords Commissioners of the Admiralty—Dam my eyes if I understand your lingo or long Proclamations, but in short give us our Due at Once and no more at it, till we go in search of the Rascals the Enemies of our Country. Henry Long. On Board His Majesty's Ship *Champion*.

For his part, Parker proposed to starve the city into compliance by preventing any shipping from passing up or down the river.

In order to maintain morale on board, effigies of Pitt were hung at the yard-arm, and there was even talk of handing the fleet over to the Dutch. To which the men on board such ships as the *Nassau*, who resented Parker's continual speechmaking, replied: 'No, we'll be damned if we leave Old England whatever happens to us.'

What in the end broke Parker's control over his Floating Republic was shortage of food and water. To the last he continued his progresses round the fleet, accompanied by bands and making speeches continually alongside every ship in turn; but on board the *Ardent*, for example, he was accused of lining his pockets with the subscriptions collected by the seamen. 'That is false', he shouted, his voice now hoarse with the efforts he was making to retain control. 'The fact is I owe my washer-woman eighteen pence, and have not money to pay her.' This remark was greeted with jeers: 'Why, then, you're a precious admiral indeed!'

On June 9 the *Leopard* slipped her cables to escape upstream under the leadership of her first lieutenant, her captain, as was the case with most of them, having been put on shore. She was followed by the *Repulse* which received a smart fire from other ships when she took the ground. As she floated off with the tide, Parker shook his fist at her, shouting, 'Damn her, she's off!'

On board the *Nassau* opinion was evenly divided. 'Our people are very dissatisfied, one half against the other', writes Hardy that day. 'One say to obey the officers, the other will hold out for their grievances, so that I may expect, and do expect, bloody work on board of us among themselves.' But the next morning he continues: 'Everything goes well at present and I am in better spirits than I have been since the breaking out of this mutiny, and I imagine it has come to its height and will end in a short time. Last night we were in a continual alarm, for two line-of-battle ships, the *Repulse* and *Leopard* slipt their cable and lowered down the flag and ran through the fleet with the intention of escaping, who kept firing at them. . . . It was the most melancholy sight I ever saw—Englishmen murdering Englishmen! The *Ardent*, another line-of-battle ship, ran into harbour this morning, after having poured her whole broadside into the ship that attempted to stop her, and got clear off. Our people are all in an uproar and fear they will be left in the lurch, but I cleared their minds on that subject and went and spoke to the principal delegates, telling them that if they returned to their duty and got under weigh I and every officer on board would do our endeavours to get her in safe, and if fired on we would all go to quarters and return their fire as fast as possible.'

Such efforts at peacemaking prevailed. The next morning the Red Flag was hauled down and all was quiet. Boats were manned to persuade other ships to do the same. All did so, except the *Sandwich* and one other. Preparations were then made to sink the flagship at her moorings, but early on June 13 Parker surrendered.

Hardy concludes with a tribute to his own men:

> I must say our people deserve the highest applause for their conduct and as it certainly was the *Nassau* led away the North Sea Fleet by being the first ship who disobeyed their officers, and the first that prevailed on the other ships to return to their duty and allegiance, and we have the credit of bringing the North Sea Fleet to a sense of their error. One half of this fleet does not want to be paid off and only came to sea to assist the *Nassau* and would follow her in everything she did or would do. . . .
>
> The conduct and bravery of our men last night has given me and all the officers a convincing proof of our ship's attachment to their Country, and would live or die for so brave a lot of men, and hope we shall have the opportunity of showing our country what men they are.

That opportunity was provided four months later at the battle of Camperdown, where seven of these mutinous ships (*Ardent, Belliqueux, Director, Isis, Montague, Lancaster, Monmouth*) behaved at the hardest-fought battle in the war as if nothing had happened to mar their discipline.

This was partly on account of the unusual humanity shown by the authorities after the mutiny had collapsed. On board the *Nassau* twenty men were court martialled, but all save one was pardoned. Only twenty-nine men were executed in the whole fleet, among them, of course, Richard Parker, who was hanged at the yard-arm of the *Sandwich*.

His Dying Declaration is an exceedingly curious document. He swore that he had been forced into the position of leader against his will and concluded—

'Remember never to make yourself the busybody of the lower classes, for they are cowardly, selfish and ungrateful; the least trifle will intimidate them, and him whom they have exalted one moment as their Demagogue, the next they will not scruple to exalt upon the gallows. I own it is with pain that I make such a remark to you, but truth demands it. I have experimentally proved it, and very soon am to be made an example of it. There is nothing new in my treatment; compare it with the treatment of the Advocates for the improvement of the conditions of the Multitude in all ages. Nay, with reverence I write it, with the treatment of Jesus Christ Himself when on earth, and then declare whether or not my advice is to be regarded.'

There is a macabre interest in what happened to his body after it had been cut down. It was buried at Sheerness, but his wife secretly exhumed it, intending to reinter it at his home near Exeter. The cart in which she was taking the body was searched on Tower Hill when she went into a tavern to get a drink. The body was then removed to a churchyard in Whitechapel, where a pupil of the famous surgeon John Hunter took a death mask (reproduced as fig. 19), which is still preserved in the Hunterian Museum of the Royal College of Surgeons of England.

7

The Blockade of the Dutch

'IMAGINE A MAN upwards of six feet four inches in height, with limbs of proportionate frame and strength. His features are nobly beautiful, his forehead high and fair, and his hair as white as snow. His movements are all stately and unaffected, and his manner easy though dignified.'

Such is the impression Admiral Adam Duncan made on a man who saw him a few months after the battle of Camperdown. He was then sixty-six years of age and still a magnificent figure of a man. In his younger days he was called the most handsome lieutenant in the Navy and it is said that the people of Chatham (the women, at least) used to crowd to their windows to see him pass down the street. Nevertheless he had to wait fifty years before he was given the opportunity to win the fame to which his modest and sterling character entitled him.

This amiable giant was born in Scotland in 1731, the son of the Provost of Dundee. His eldest brother died when an officer in the East India Company, whose marine service carried almost as high a social prestige as the Royal Navy. The second brother joined the Army to become the Major Duncan of Fenimore Cooper's novel of the French wars in Canada, *The Pathfinder*. It was said of him that 'wherever he went, a respectable library went with him'. Clearly, an unusual army officer in those days.

Adam, the third son, joined the Navy at the age of fifteen. For the next half-century he followed the usual stages of a naval career, seeing plenty of action in the intervals of long spells 'on the beach', but never finding an opportunity to distinguish himself above his brother officers. Purely by accident he followed Keppel's star, though there is no indication that he ever shared his political views.

He served under Keppel as midshipman, lieutenant and flag captain. As a post-captain it so happened that his ship was at Spithead when Keppel was court martialled after the battle of Ushant in 1778, so that he had a seat on the board. By another coincidence he was also a member of the board which tried and acquitted Keppel's rival, Sir Hugh Palliser.

Duncan's professional record was of sound rather than brilliant service. At the end of the Seven Years' War he led a storming-party at the capture of Havana and took a captain's share of the unprecedented amount of prize money which was distributed afterwards. He was a captain at thirty, but was not promoted admiral until he was fifty-six and then did not fly his flag until ten years later when, in 1795, he was appointed to command the North Sea station.

One of the reasons for his slow promotion to the highest rank was the fever which he contracted at Havana, which compelled him to decline further service in tropical areas. It was this which made him refuse the command of the Mediterranean fleet in 1795, a command which went, as we have seen, to Sir John Jervis. It was indeed partly on Duncan's advice that this appointment was made. He had succeeded Jervis in command of the *Foudroyant* in 1783 and naturally when he found her the most efficient ship afloat he entertained the highest regard for the professional merits of his predecessor. Having declined the Mediterranean command, he was asked whom he considered the most suitable officer for that service. 'Beyond all doubt it was Sir John Jervis', he told Pitt and Spencer. Curiously enough, he again succeeded Old Jarvie in command of the *Foudroyant* in 1799.

Although ill health may have caused him to refuse important commands, his connection by marriage with the powerful Dundas interest put him in a strong position when the war against the French Revolution broke out. In 1777 he married Henrietta, daughter of Robert Dundas, Lord Arniston, a name to be execrated in Scotland because of his reactionary views when he was a leading figure of the judiciary. His wife was thus the niece of Henry Dundas, now both Treasurer of the Navy and Secretary of State for War. A hitherto unpublished letter by Dundas to his niece, written (or rather scrawled) immediately after the news of her husband's victory reached London, throws a pleasant light on their relationship:

Do you remember, my dear Mrs. Duncan, when you first conceived your attachment to the admiral when Captain Duncan, and applied to me to speak to your Father, that before doing so I made it a special condition that you would never directly nor indirectly use any influence to induce him to give over his profession? Do you now repent that I made that condition and that you made that promise? God bless you, my dear, your husband has gained immortal glory and done more signal service to his country than ever any man had it in his power to do. In place of being an Irish Peeress [as was promised in 1796] don't be surprised to learn in a few days that you are his countess in the British House of Lords. My love to all the family. Mr. Pitt and I are going down to Walmer this evening, but if we hear that the admiral is got to the Nore, it is our intention to visit him tomorrow morning on board the *Venerable*. I remain, my dear Mrs. Duncan, your very loving

HENRY DUNDAS.

There is a family tradition that when Spencer and Dundas were going through the list of admirals at the beginning of the war, the former exclaimed 'What can be the reason that Keppel's Duncan has never been brought forward?' The same night he was appointed commander-in-chief of the North Sea station. The trouble about the story is that at that date Spencer was not yet First Lord. But it may well be true of February 1795, when Duncan was actually appointed, and it is certain that he owed the post largely to his interest with Dundas.

The North Sea command stretched from Selsey Bill in Sussex to Cape Wrath in Scotland. Its title was more substantial than the number of ships Duncan was given to guard such a length of coastline. He began with only four sail of the line, but by the date of the battle this had been increased to 16. However, his fleet was never the homogeneous force which Jervis commanded in the Mediterranean. It consisted of the oldest and least seaworthy ships in commission and it is significant that the flagship was called the *Venerable* because this old and ill-found 74 leaked incessantly, the rain even penetrating the admiral's cabin: on the day of battle he had serious doubts if she could keep afloat. Many of the ships stationed at Nore belonged to his fleet, though this was a separate command. All of them were manned by the refuse of London, pressed men and even Greenwich pensioners. The ships were of all shapes and sizes—

ex-East Indiamen, converted prizes, old frigates and brigs which were constantly being set off on detached services, such as escorting Baltic convoys across the North Sea, chasing off Dunkirk privateers or protecting Greenland fishing fleets. We need not wonder so much at the fact that mutiny broke out in this fleet as at Duncan's gift of leadership that made it fight so well at Camperdown.

His duty for the two years preceding the battle was the close blockade of the 20-odd ships of the Dutch fleet in the Texel. This was performed in the strictest manner by the scratch lot of ships at his disposal. Every day, in all weathers, winter and summer, his scouting craft looked into the Texel to report on the state of the enemy to the main fleet anchored either in the Downs or off Yarmouth. The Admiralty was always promising reinforcements, but it was seldom as good as its word, because the North Sea fleet was regarded as of minor importance compared with the Channel fleet off Brest or with the Mediterranean fleet off Cadiz.

The only notable addition to Duncan's strength was the arrival of 12 Russian ships and 6 frigates under Admirals Honickoff, Mackaroff and Tate in the summer of 1795. The last named was of Scottish descent, as were many in the Empress Catherine's navy. Though they usually returned to the Baltic during the winter months, when the blockade of the Dutch coast was most unpleasant, some of the ships remained with Duncan for the next two years and it was quite fortuitous that none were present at the battle in October 1797.

Their number was considerable, but their use was small. The Empress Catherine's navy was never an efficient force. The health of the men was notoriously bad, because they were ill fed and disgustingly dirty in their habits, so that scurvy and typhus took full toll of their numbers. All the niceties of protocol had to be observed, producing endless opportunities for friction. The Russian officers were not accustomed to British methods of signalling or tactics, so that Duncan probably felt fortunate in not having such an unreliable force with him on the day of battle.

The extraordinary thing is that five years after the battle the Russians put in a claim for a share of the prizes. From Duncan's unpublished correspondence with his prize agents we can see what a burden the Russians really were when they were operating with his fleet. He says that he will not make his complaints public unless the Russians press their claims, but in fact they had not a leg to stand on, because no arrangements had ever been entered into regarding the distribution of prize money, nor had they ever regarded themselves as under his command, since they refused to salute his flag during the months preceding the battle. They had never captured an enemy vessel, nor even stopped a neutral to examine her for contraband. After Duncan's ships deserted him during the weeks of the mutiny, he considered Mackaroff's behaviour 'shabby' when he sailed away without the admiral's consent, leaving him totally unsupported. He concludes: 'Shall strangers and foreigners who profited so much and improved in naval tactics while under Lord Duncan, but rendered him no material service, pluck his prize money out of his pocket?'

What with the problem of keeping the Russians in a good temper, victualling their ships, caring for their sick and at the same time blockading the Dutch with his exiguous forces, it is not surprising that Duncan sometimes complained to the Admiralty that even his stout shoulders could not bear the burden indefinitely. In November 1795, he told the First Lord: 'I am the first British admiral that was ever ordered on service with foreigners only, and I must beg further to say I shall look upon it as an indignity to me if *some* British ships are not directed to attend me.'

To which Spencer, sitting by the fire at Admiralty House, could only reply 'The defects of the *Venerable* do not seem very material at present and cannot afford any grounds of objection to a cruise not intended to be of long continuance. Notwithstanding the convoy from Elsinore which has already sailed, we have information of a large number more that are still waiting to come from thence, and the news of our ships being disabled in the North Sea [the *Repulse* having carried away her main yard] may make the Dutch fleet feel a little bolder.'

Which meant that not only were no reinforcements forthcoming, but that more ships would be detached for escort purposes, so that Duncan was left to carry on the blockade chiefly with Russian assistance, if such it could be called. No wonder he got Dundas to suggest that at his age a comfortable seat on the Board might be preferable to beating up and down the Dutch coast in all weathers; but again Spencer replied abruptly: 'The services of Admiral Duncan are so valuable in the situation in which he now acts that he could not possibly be spared from it.'

So, while Jervis was training the Mediterranean fleet into a first-rate weapon of war, Duncan strove to keep together his scratch lot of ships. His officers were constantly changing as their ships were sent off on detached services, which made fleet manœuvres impossible. None the less, this is how his vice-admiral describes the way in which the blockade was maintained: 'The cutters as near the Texel as they can safely get, the frigates next them, then two line-of-battle ships to cover them, and the rest of us without and still farther off so as to be seen from their lookout. This keeps them in suspense as to the amount of our force. Today we make a grand display.'

By that date Duncan had seventeen ships of all rates under his command, whereas the Dutch had 16 sail of the line and 12 frigates. None the less Dundas decided that an army should be landed on the Continent. At the same time a naval officer suggested a fireship attack on the Texel fleet. The admiral had no difficulty in showing the latter that there was no chance of a successful attack during the winter months, but the proposed expedition to the Helder still held good in spite of his adverse comments. He faithfully went ahead organising his fleet in the support role, sensibly ending his instructions to his captains with the words: 'It is the admiral's intention not to make any more signals than are absolutely necessary.' The ships and troops were actually off the Dutch coast when the whole thing was postponed on account of bad weather.

Three years later just such an expedition was launched with Anglo-Russian troops under the command of the Duke of York and General Sir Ralph Abercrombie. Duncan, who was still in command of the North Sea Fleet, was the senior admiral of the fleet of 250 transports. After the landing had been made, 13 Dutch warships and 3 Indiamen, which were lying in the Nieuwe Deep, surrendered without firing a shot. A few days later another 12, including some of those which had escaped destruction in 1797, surrendered in the Texel. Apart from the laxness of Admiral Storij's behaviour, the only explanation of this extraordinary action on the part of men who fought so well at Camperdown is that offered by the contemporary historian James: 'The fact is the sailors had become politicians; and, differing in opinion from their officers, had adopted a course which, if not the most honourable, was under present circumstances undoubtedly the most safe. They mutinied and refused to fight; and as if fearful that the guns would go off by themselves, they in many cases drew the charges and threw the shot overboard.'

Perhaps Duncan, after his own experiences, was in a position to sympathise with Admiral Storij's predicament; but we can be sure that if a French landing had been made at Yarmouth in 1797, neither the mutineers nor the admiral would have behaved in so abject a fashion.

The military part of the expedition was, however, a complete failure. The Duke's troops were expelled so ignominiously that it inspired the well-known song about 'The grand old Duke of York. . . .' Nearly 5000 casualties were suffered and few of the Dutch prizes proved seaworthy. Four British frigates were wrecked on that difficult coast, one of them the 32-gun *Lutine* which was carrying money for the payment of the troops. She was salvaged and her bell is the principal historic relic at Lloyd's today.

To return to 1797, when the blockade was intensified as news filtered through about preparations for an invasion from the region of Dunkirk. The Dutch fleet would obviously be called upon to cover the crossing, so Duncan tightened his hold upon the Texel. The news of the victory off Cape St. Vincent reached him from Spencer in these words: 'Sir John Jervis with 15 of the line has just beat 27 Spaniards and taken 4 of their best ships; I hope soon to be able to congratulate you upon as brilliant a day.' Since Duncan had been largely instrumental in getting Jervis appointed, he must have felt that the event justified his judgement. And when a smuggler-spy named Richard Cadman Etches warned that something fresh was intended against the coasts of Essex and Suffolk, Duncan could reply with confidence that 'the late glorious victory may for a time damp the ardour of all our enemies.'

However, he was kept on the alert by the following letter from the First Lord on April 10: 'I hope you will have been able to keep your station in this easterly wind, as our secret informer on the Continent mentions this very day as the day fixed for the Dutch fleet to sail, and the wind, if they choose it, is as fair as possible for them to come out; their destination is said to be an attack on Jersey or Guernsey, but I cannot say I give much credit to it.'

20   The *'Active'* cutter bringing Duncan news that the Dutch fleet is at sea
From an aquatint by E. Duncan after W. J. Huggins

21   The *'Vrijheid'* receiving a final broadside from the *'Director'*
From a watercolour by Samuel Owen

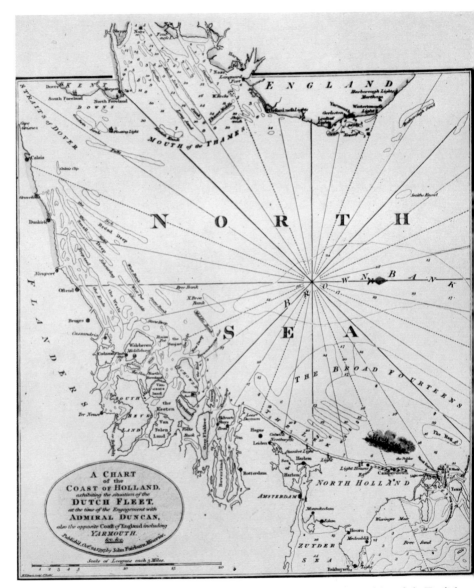

22   *Chart by W. T. Davis showing the battle of Camperdown (bottom right) and the English coast near Yarmouth (top right)*

Then the mutinies intervened and Duncan, as we have seen, was driven to the necessity of blockading the Texel with only two ships making signals to an imaginary fleet over the horizon. His tactics were the same as during the preceding twelve months, but now there was no fleet to implement them: now there was nothing but the admiral in the *Venerable* and his vice-admiral, Richard Onslow, in the *Adamant*, his own ship having mutinied.

Duncan's opponent, Admiral John William de Winter, was a much younger man, but of the same stamp and size. After the battle Winter remarked that it was surprising that two such gigantic objects as himself and the English admiral should have escaped unscathed from the carnage of the day. He entered the Dutch navy in 1762 as a boy of twelve (Duncan was then a captain of thirty-one). He had only reached the rank of lieutenant when the French Revolution broke out and a fundamental difference began to appear between him and the English admiral. There is no evidence that Duncan ever entertained any pronounced political opinions, but the life of a sea officer on the Continent in those days was very different. De Winter sympathised deeply with the aims of the Revolution. As a patriotic republican, he was opposed to Dutch monarchical sentiments and therefore ended his naval career in order to go into exile in France. There he served in the Revolutionary army when war broke out and thus re-entered Holland as a general when the French overran that country in 1795 to set up the Batavian Republic. It was on that occasion that a regiment of cavalry captured the Dutch fleet as it lay ice-bound in the Zuyder Zee—the only occasion in history when soldiers have captured ships.

De Winter reverted to his former profession when he was appointed admiral in command of the Texel fleet, though he had never commanded a ship before. The Stadtholder having fled to England, the names of many of the Dutch ships were altered in accordance with the spirit of the times: the flagship was now the *Vrijheid* (Liberty) and other ships bore names like *Gelijkheid* (Equality) *States General, Brutus,* etc. They were stout, well-built ships of a shallow draft and, at least in respect of frigates, more numerous than their English blockaders. But it was never a homogeneous force, because the Dutch bore the French yoke uneasily. There was widespread sympathy with the House of Orange, now in exile, in spite of the admiral's republican views. The Dutch got nothing out of the French alliance: indeed, they suffered heavily in respect of their colonial possessions as soon as Britain declared war. Their principal squadron overseas was defeated by Vice-Admiral Elphinstone (later Lord Keith) at Saldanha Bay, a victory which achieved the first conquest of the Cape of Good Hope. It was from this victory that Elphinstone was returning at the end of 1796 when he found himself involved in the Bantry Bay operations.

Moreover the Dutch were naturally proud of their naval tradition, especially in encounters with the British. The whole coastline running south from the Texel was dominated by the shades of De Ruyter, Martin and Cornelius Van Tromp. More recently their fleet had acquitted itself well at the battle of the Dogger Bank in 1781. What a contrast with French naval history! If they were to fight against France's enemy by sea, they preferred to do so alone. Looking at the state of the French navy after the purges of the Revolution, they were justifiably sceptical about its efficiency. Therein lay the seeds of the delays and disasters of the next two years, leading ultimately to the ignominious surrender of 1799.

However, in the summer of 1797 everything seemed ripe for a successful conclusion of the war on the part of France and her allies. Bantry Bay might have proved a fiasco, and the Spanish fleet was now out of action, but on land French troops carried all before them. Bonaparte was triumphant in Italy, Moreau on the Rhine, Hoche was winning a series of victories as commander of the army of Sambre-et-Meuse. The situation was similar to that which prevailed in the summer of 1940, when German arms seemed invincible and Britain stood alone and apparently prostrate. Bantry Bay had at least stirred the United Irishmen into activity and in the spring came the news of the mutinies in the British fleet.

To Wolfe Tone, now on the staff of General Daendels, the commander-in-chief of the Dutch army, the opportunity for invasion seemed obvious. Even the French Minister of Marine was anxious not to miss it. On June 21 he wrote (somewhat belatedly, for the mutinies were nearly over) to Hoche suggesting the despatch of 16,000 Dutch troops under Daendels and 6000 French troops from Brest for another attack on Ireland. The expedition might be covered by Winter's fleet which, he said had 'long been ready for sea'. Both Hoche and Tone agreed, so that the latter was sent to Holland to settle matters with the Dutch. In his diary he expresses pleasure at the forwardness of preparations which he found there, the high morale of the troops and the efficiency of the Dutch naval armament in contrast with what he had experienced at Brest.

He was given a cabin on board the *Vrijheid*, but from that moment everything went wrong. British fleets were once more blockading Brest and Texel. The wind turned contrary and for a month continued to blow from the west, thus preventing the ships from leaving their anchorage. The British were well apprised of the situation, judging from Duncan's letter to Spencer of July 18:

> *Venerable*, at sea, Texel east fifteen miles. Intelligence received yesterday that the Dutch fleet unmoored intending to put to sea with 30,000 troops embarked in transports and in their ships of war and that a French general had arrived that day and was saluted on going on board the fleet. We distinctly heard them salute. Their Lordships being in possession of their number and force, must know how inadequate the force I have is to theirs, and although I have no doubt of giving a very good account of them in the event of an action, yet, from their great superiority of numbers, their frigates and transports may proceed on their intended expedition without my being able to prevent it.

But at the same time he received a touching assurance of the loyalty of his men, now that the last embers of the mutiny had been stamped out. An anonymous letter from the captains of the foretops thanked the merchants of Yarmouth for their offer of a gift of porter and concluded:

> We cannot omit this opportunity to express our gratitude and affection to you, our Commander-in-Chief, for your paternal care, attention and salutary advice in every stage of that unhappy event which has stained the character of the British tar, but which we hope and trust may be redeemed by future bravery and a steady perseverance in their country's cause. We sincerely wish the enemy may give us an opportunity of manifesting our loyalty to our King, our steady attachment to the Constitution, and our personal regard for the best of Commanders.

We can follow the sequence of events from the enemy's point of view in Wolfe Tone's diary for the next month.

'*July 14.* The report today is that we shall get under way tomorrow and I see a bustle in the ship which seems to confirm it; but I follow my good old rule, to ask no questions. Several boats full of troops have passed us today going on board different vessels; the men are in the highest spirits, singing national songs and cheering the General as they pass; it is a noble sight and I found it inexpressedly affecting. . . .

'*July 18.* The wind is as foul as possible this morning; it cannot be worse. Hell! Hell! Hell! Allah! Allah! I am in a most devouring rage.

'*July 19.* Admiral De Winter and I endeavour to pass away the time playing the flute, which he does very well; we have some good duets and that is some relief. It is, however, impossible to conceive anything more irksome than waiting, as we now are, on the wind; what is still worse, the same wind that locks us up here is exactly favourable for the arrival of reinforcements for Duncan, if Lord Spencer means to send him any. Our ships exercise at the great guns and small arms every day; they fire in general incomparably well and it is a noble spectacle. . . .

'*August 2.* Everything goes on here from bad to worse and I am tormented and unhappy more than I can express. On the 30th in the morning early the wind was fair, the signal given to prepare to get under way and everything ready, when, at the very instant we were about to weigh anchor and put to sea, the wind chopped about and left us. . . . There seems to be a fate in this business. Five weeks, I believe six weeks [actually eight] the English fleet lay paralysed by the mutinies at Portsmouth, Plymouth and the Nore. The sea was open and nothing to prevent both the Dutch and the French fleets to put to sea. Well, nothing was ready; that precious opportunity which we can never expect to return was lost; and now that at last we are ready here, the wind is against us, the mutiny is quelled and we are sure to be attacked by a superior force. At Brest it is, I fancy, still worse. Had we been in Ireland at the time of the insurrection of the Nore, we should beyond a doubt have had at least that fleet, and God only knows the influence such an event might have had on the whole British navy. The destiny of Europe might have been changed for ever; but, as I have said, the great occasion is lost, and we must do as well as we can.

'*August 8.* We have now been detained so long that our hopes of undertaking the expedition to Ireland are beginning exceedingly to relax, and I more than suspect the General is speculating on one elsewhere.'

He was quite right. De Winter and Daendels had given up all idea of passing the fleet down-Channel, and the French Minister of Marine was having second thoughts about the wisdom of employing the Dutch. Duncan had been almost glad to see the troops embarking because he knew that, as long as the wind held, disease and privation would soon do their work in those over-crowded holds. It was the exhaustion of provisions that finally decided De Winter to insist on disembarkation. He still hoped for a smaller expedition of 2500 men, but Daendels refused to risk it unless the number was at least 4000.

A new plan was suggested to Tone and at the end of August he was sent back to Paris to win Hoche's approval. This was that De Winter should offer battle and, if victorious, 15,000 Dutch troops would be landed at Edinburgh to march across to Glasgow. The fleet could be passed through the Forth–Clyde canal and the troops could then be ferried across to northern Ireland. De Winter was not impressed. No seaman could approve of such a plan on professional grounds, and even Hoche was sceptical.

On arrival at Paris, Tone found himself in the middle of a political crisis, as a result of which Hoche and others were dismissed by the Directory. Though only twenty-nine years old, the general was in an advanced state of tuberculosis, of which he died on September 19. Napoleon wrote his epitaph: 'One of the ablest generals ever produced by France. The ideal wager of war.' Who knows if the two men might not have developed as rivals?

Tone remained unhappily at Paris, out of touch with events until the news of Camperdown arrived. 'It was well that I was not on board the *Vrijheid*. If I had, it would have been a pretty piece of business. I fancy I am not to be caught at sea by the English, for this is the second escape I have had; and by land I mock myself of them.'

He did not escape a third time. Continuing his intrigues for another landing in Ireland, however small, he sailed on board the *Hoche* early in 1798, once more under the name of General Smith. The ship was intercepted off Ulster by a squadron under the command of Sir John Borlase Warren. Wolfe Tone was recognised among the prisoners taken. He was condemned to be hanged at Dublin, but before the English could execute him he cut his throat with a penknife in prison. In the long line of Irish patriots, we cannot say that he was the noblest of them all, but he was certainly the most optimistic and his diary reveals him as the most human and perhaps the most tragic.

8

The Battle of Camperdown

EARLY ON THE morning of October 9 the *Speculator* lugger appeared under press of sail at the back of Yarmouth sands with the urgent news that the Dutch were at sea. Within a few hours Duncan was able to send a message to the Admiralty: 'The wind is now at NE and [I] shall make good course over to them, and if it please God, hope to get at them. The Squadron under my command are unmoored and I shall put to sea immediately.'

Just over a week earlier he had anchored off Yarmouth after a cruise lasting nineteen weeks. So long a time at sea had been rendered imperative partly because of the rumours of impending invasion, partly because it was thought advisable to give the crews a good shake-down at sea, now that the mutinies were over. It was high summer, so that the buffetings by easterly gales which he had experienced in the spring no longer worried him. But the cruise was of sufficient duration to bring on scorbutic symptoms, even among some of the officers. The ships were foul and strained by continual cruising. Nevertheless, as soon as he reached Yarmouth he told his officers in what *The Times* called his 'plain and affable way': 'I shall not, gentlemen, put foot out of the ship. Your supplies of water and provisions shall be sent to you in the morning, and I hope to be able to sail again in twenty hours, when an early meeting with the enemy will give us cause to rejoice. To complete my wishes, the caulkers shall go over my ship's bows in the morning and do their best to keep her afloat.'

Now the moment he had anticipated for the past two years was come. At noon on the 9th he sailed with eleven of his line-of-battle ships, leaving the others to catch him up at sea. Two of them—the *Russell* (74) and *Adamant* (64)—had been left with the *Circe* frigate and some cutters to blockade the enemy coast under Captain Trollope.

The *Speculator*'s news was confirmed a few hours later by the *Vestal* and *Active* cutters (see illustration 20), which described Trollope's movements during the past three days in more detail. It appeared that De Winter with 16 sail of the line, 5 frigates and 5 brigs, had left the Texel on October 7. As they came out they tried to chase Trollope off station, but he had given them the slip and had shadowed them for the next forty-eight hours. Their course appeared to be SW, so that it looked as if they intended to cross over to England and not go northabout on some invasion business.

What no one could understand was why De Winter had ever put to sea and what he was doing cruising down the Dutch coast. According to English intelligence, invasion plans were past history, now that Hoche was dead. Wolfe Tone in Paris was equally at a loss. To him it seemed 'direct treason' to put to sea at that time of year 'without motives or object'. De Winter's own explanation when a prisoner is bald enough: that he was ordered to put to sea against his will by the naval committee at the Hague 'to show they had done so'. From Dutch sources we know that his instructions, dated October 5, were to put to sea as soon as the wind was favourable and 'when at sea act according to Articles 9, 10, 11 of the Instructions given on July 10', that is to say when an Irish invasion plan was in the air. These articles instructed him to offer battle if there was any chance of success, bearing in mind the way Dutch admirals in the past had maintained the honour of the flag (as if anyone in the Dutch navy was likely to forget it): 'In case of an approaching engagement to try and draw the enemy as near the harbours of the Republic as will be found possible in conformity with the rules of prudence and strategy.'

But why were such orders reissued in October? No satisfactory answer has ever been given to the question. It certainly had nothing to do with an invasion scheme at that particular date, though it must be remembered that such schemes continued to be entertained until Bonaparte was appointed to the Army of England next spring, when he took one look at the Channel and then stated flatly: 'To make a descent upon England without being masters of the sea is the boldest and most difficult operation ever attempted'; and then turned his eyes east to Egypt. We know that De Winter himself was against the plan, but it seems that the naval committee was basking in the

23 *Admiral Lord Duncan*
From the painting by H. P. Danloux

24   *The Battle of Camperdown*

Showing the 'Vrijheid' on left, 'Venerable' and 'Hercules' in centre

From an aquatint by T. Hellyer after T. Whitcombe

traditional glories of De Ruyter and were convinced that Duncan's fleet could be beaten. Motives of prestige, always the most dangerous in such thinking, can be the only explanation of an action which was strategically irrelevant.

De Winter had only progressed some forty miles along the coast when, on October 10, he heard from a fishing vessel that Duncan was at sea. As he himself had always doubted the capabilities of his fleet, and had never commanded a ship in battle, he decided to run for home. In so doing he prepared to lay the trap for the British which his instructions suggested. Dutch ships were of shallow draft because of the surrounding seas. If he could steal along the coast through the shallows, he might be able to lure Duncan on to a lee shore, where the possibilities of shipwreck were very considerable.

But he overlooked two things—the high standard of seamanship which any fleet constantly at sea must achieve; and the excellence of British gunnery, which enabled them to fire three rounds to the enemy's two. Moreover, the British ships were armed with 86 carronades, a murderous upper deck weapon at close range, whereas the Dutch had none. What made the battle such a 'damned close run thing', as Wellington said on another occasion, was that the two fleets were as evenly matched in point of numbers as they were in the stoutness of their ships and in the courage of their hearts. The Dutch had the advantage of position and the number of frigates. The British were better trained at sea, and it is clear from the determination of the crews that they intended to erase the memories of the mutinies. For such reasons the battle was the hardest fought— Trafalgar included—of all during that long war at sea, and the casualties were higher in proportion.

The fresh north-east wind blew Duncan directly towards the Dutch coast. After a fine morning, the sky clouded over, there were squalls of rain, so that visibility was poor. The captain of the *Circe* frigate was the first to sight the enemy, because he climbed up to the maintop to catch a glimpse of their sails above the horizon. He signalled the admiral that the enemy was nine miles away to the south-east between the villages of Egmont and Camperdown, the Texel bearing north-east fifteen miles. The Dutch were then about five miles from the shore in a mere nine fathoms of water, so that hundreds of spectators on the sand dunes could see the fury of the battle, although the smoke and rain prevented them from distinguishing the details.

Duncan came on deck at dawn on October 12 after as good a night's sleep as he had ever enjoyed in his life. He was exhilarated by the prospect of a battle which would terminate the long, dull months of blockade. As the *Venerable* drove under full sail towards the Dutch coast in the van of the fleet, which was in no distinct order, the admiral took the opportunity of summoning his officers on deck 'and in their presence prostrated himself in prayer before the God of Hosts'.

One story, which must be apocryphal, is that he told them that as they saw a hard winter approaching they had best keep up a good fire. Another, which sounds more in character, is that when he saw a thirteen-year-old midshipman ducking his head as the ship came under fire, he patted the boy on the back saying: 'Very well, my boy, but don't do it again. You might put your head in the way of a shot.'

The following letter by Duncan's aunt, which has not been printed before, adds some typical touches. As the admiral paced the quarter-deck, he was asked how many ships he proposed to engage when the battle was joined. "'Really, sir, I can't ascertain, but when we have beat them we will count them.' Ordering the pilot to advance he (the pilot) said the water was so shallow he was afraid to run aground. 'Go on at your peril', said the gallant admiral, 'for I am determined to fight the ships on land if I cannot by sea.' When the battle was over, he called up the clergyman and made all in his ship that were able return thanks to God Almighty for all his mercies showered upon them and him. After that they refreshed themselves. This, they say, was never done before under these circumstances."

The tactics employed by Duncan on his approach are of great interest because they seem at first sight to prefigure those employed by Nelson at Trafalgar. That is to say, an approach in two groups (not columns, as at Trafalgar) concentrating on the centre and rear of an enemy line of battle (a much better formed line than the loose crescent of the allied fleets on October 21, 1805). But where Nelson planned his mode of attack with his captains beforehand, though the actual course of the *Victory* remained uncertain, Duncan's tactics were determined by the necessities of the situation which confronted him when he sighted the enemy at 9.0 a.m. on October 12 (October

11 in the logs, because the nautical day still ran from noon to noon). A study of the signals recorded in the logs suggests that Duncan intended at first to attack in line of bearing, so that each of his ships would come down upon her opposite number, as Collingwood's did at Trafalgar. But the urgency of joining battle before the enemy escaped forced him to change his mind and allow his ships to engage as best they could. Hence the concentration was fortuitous. The bare statement in his despatch supports this explanation: 'As we approached near, I made the signal to shorten sail in order to connect them [i.e. the slower sailing ships]; soon after, I saw the land between Camperdown and Egmont about nine miles to leeward of the enemy and, finding there was no time to be lost in making the attack, I made the signal to bear up, break the enemy line and engage them to leeward, each ship her opponent; by which I got between them and the land whither they were fast approaching.'

De Winter had begun his retreat in three columns. When he laid his trap for Duncan at about half past nine, he formed line of battle. A certain amount of confusion ensued. The *Brutus* (Rear-Admiral Bloys von Treslong) was the flagship of the rear division which now became the van, but she fell back towards the centre, leaving the van without a commander. However, except for some looseness about the centre, the Dutch line of battle was tautly formed, with the frigates and brigs to leeward in shoal water.

Duncan evidently intended to use the tactics which Howe adopted on the Glorious First of June, that is to say to form line of bearing and break the enemy's line at all points. Thus his first signal at 9.22 was to form line on a starboard bearing and to allow the slower ships to catch up. But the line was never formed, since he now saw that he had no time to lose. By 11.0 the faster ships had outstripped the laggards. The fleet was therefore in no sort of order beyond two well-defined groups, one headed by Vice-Admiral Richard Onslow in the *Monarch* and the other by Duncan in the *Venerable*. A series of confusing signals followed, some of which were mistakes and most of which were not taken in by the more distant ships. Thus a signal at 11.17 to take station in line was countermanded when it was realised that Trollope's ships had never seen a copy of the new order of battle. Having ordered 'General Chase', 'Bear Up and Sail Large' and, at 11.53, 'Pass Through the Enemy's Line and Engage

Plan I

CAMPERDOWN

12.30 p.m.

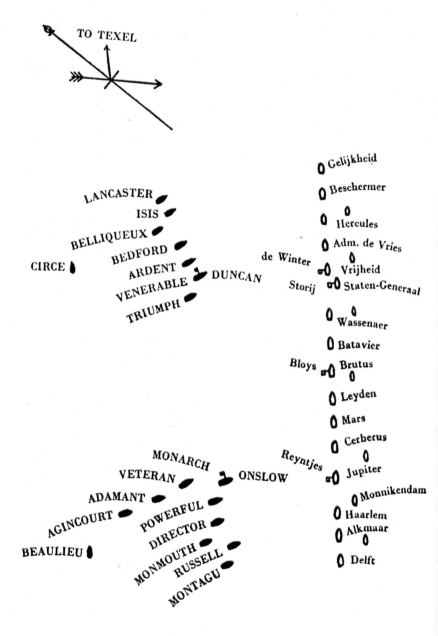

TO TEXEL

from to Leeward' (Howe's signal), Duncan let his captains do their best. The faster ships would be in action first. The rest would understand by the signal for close action, which was kept flying, that each must seek her adversary. Such proved to be the case, with the single exception of the *Agincourt* (Captain John Williamson), who was later court martialled.

The log of the *Director* (Captain William Bligh) is by far the best kept and the most informative. He describes the moment the fleet engaged thus: 'At noon our fleet standing in two divisions for action. The *Monarch, Russell, Director* and *Montagu* the headmost ships. The *Monarch* on our larboard beam standing towards the Dutch Vice-Admiral. Admiral Duncan nobly leading his division towards the Dutch Commander-in-Chief. The enemy's line formed on a wind on the larboard tack about NE by E.' (See Plan I, p. 140.)

A remark made by the captain of the *Belliqueux* probably reflects the general feeling at the confused signals from the flagship. Throwing his signal book upon the deck, Captain Inglis, a Scotsman noted for the shortness of his temper, swore 'Damn . . . . Up wi' the hel-lem and gang into the middle o' it.'

Some years later St. Vincent told his biographer that: 'Lord Duncan's action was fought pell mell, without plan or system; he was a gallant officer, but had no idea of tactics, and being soon puzzled by them, attacked without attention to form or order.' 'Pell mell' is certainly a fair description of what happened at Camperdown, but there is nothing to suggest that Duncan was any more puzzled by tactics than any other officer, and, as we have seen, his mode of approach was dominated by the time factor.

We can understand St. Vincent's remark better if we remember that it was made in the context of denying the claims of James Clerk of Eldin that his *Essay on Naval Tactics* (1782) was responsible for all the major victories of that epoch because he, a civilian, taught the admirals that the key to victory was to break the enemy's line. We may sympathise with St. Vincent's impatience at what looked like Scottish arrogance; but what he did not know was that Duncan as a captain had met Clerk at Edinburgh and owned a well-thumbed copy of his book. In a pamphlet published later to promote his claims, Clerk said that he met Duncan again after the battle of Camperdown, when the admiral 'acknowledged in person to Mr.

Clerk how much he was indebted for the victory to his Tactics', and assisted Clerk in preparing a plan of the battle.

The truth of the matter is best summarised by something which De Winter said to Duncan after his defeat: 'Your not waiting to form line ruined me: if I had got nearer the shore and you had attacked, I should probably have drawn both fleets on it, and it would have been a victory for me, being on my own coast.'

The action began when the *Jupiter* (Rear-Admiral Reyntjes) opened fire on the *Monarch*, Onslow's flagship in the weather division of the British line, when she came within range at 12.30. The *Monarch* withheld her fire until she was in a raking position between the *Jupiter*, lying fourth from the Dutch rear, and the *Haarlem*, lying third. Onslow then fired both broadsides with devastating effect. But she was brought up short when the *Monniken-dam* frigate gallantly and unexpectedly threw herself in her way. The frigate, in her turn, suffered the full blast of the *Monarch*'s second broadside, so that her steering wheel was shot away and she drifted to leeward of the Dutch rear. There she continued the fight until fifty of her crew were killed, sixty wounded and the ship was filling fast. She struck at last, but later became a total wreck.

The concentration of Onslow's attack enabled him to bring nine ships against five of the Dutch. All the latter, except the *Alkmaar*, surrendered within the next hour—the *Jupiter*, *Haarlem*, *Delft* and *Monnikendam*. Rear-Admiral Reyntjes died of his wounds, as did a third of the men under his command. Rear-Admiral Meures was taken prisoner.

Soon after Onslow had opened the British attack, Duncan in the *Venerable*, leading the lee division and closely supported by the *Triumph* and *Ardent*, struck at the *Vrijheid*, the Dutch flagship lying fifth from the van. But he was unable to break the enemy line at his first blow because the *States General* (Rear-Admiral Storij) moved up to close the gap. He therefore put his helm aport and ran under the latter's stern to give her such a battering that she was forced out of the line, though she continued in action.

A similar concentration to that achieved in the rear now developed on the Dutch van, where the *Bedford* engaged the *De Vries* ahead of the *Vrijheid*, and the *Belliqueux*, *Lancaster* and *Isis* attacked the leading ships. The situation around the *Vrijheid* soon became extremely

CAMPERDOWN
1.0 p.m.

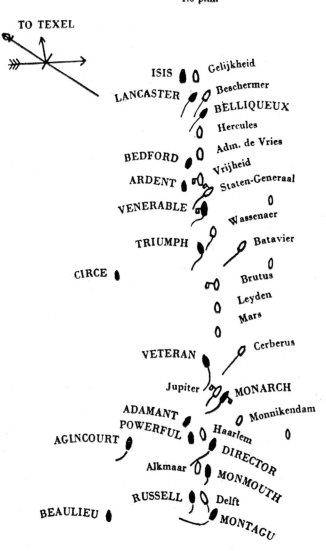

TO TEXEL

ISIS   Gelijkheid

LANCASTER   Beschermer

BELLIQUEUX

Hercules

Adm. de Vries

BEDFORD

Vrijheid

ARDENT   Staten-Generaal

VENERABLE

Wassenaer

TRIUMPH   Batavier

CIRCE   Brutus

Leyden

Mars

VETERAN   Cerberus

Jupiter   MONARCH

ADAMANT   Monnikendam

POWERFUL   Haarlem

AGINCOURT   DIRECTOR

Alkmaar   MONMOUTH

RUSSELL   Delft

BEAULIEU   MONTAGU

complicated and dangerous for the *Venerable*, who found herself surrounded for the next two hours by three and sometimes four Dutch ships of similar strength. The *States General* having swung too far before the wind, the *Venerable* could now engage the *Vrijheid* from to leeward, but she found herself with the Dutch flagship to port, the *States General* to starboard, the *De Vries* ahead and the *Wassenaer* astern of her. Had not all these ships been engaged at the same time by other British ships, the *Venerable* must have been captured at the height of the battle about two o'clock. (See Plan II, p. 143.)

Help was on the way. The *Triumph*'s log admits that she was 'much cut up' in her first attack on the *De Vries*, but a lucky shot from her quarter-deck carronade hit a powder cask on board the *Hercules* next to her. A fire immediately started on deck, spread to the rigging and in a few minutes this Dutch 64 was a flaming fireship, as much a danger to her friends as to her foes. She drifted towards the shore, causing confusion to all around her, until she was secured after the general action had ended.

The *Lancaster* and *Belliqueux* were now forcing their way down the line to assist the *Venerable* and *Triumph*. The *Powerful* and *Director* were coming up astern, and the *Ardent* was still gallantly locked in combat with the *Vrijheid* on her port side. (See Plan III, p. 145.) She was only a 64 and she suffered heavier casualties as a result than any other ship that day. Had the *Agincourt* supported her, as she might have done now that she was not engaged in the rear, she would not have suffered so badly, but Williamson's ship was the only one which failed to do her duty. The captain of the *Ardent*, Richard Burgess, was killed in the first ten minutes. The master was struck down soon after, two lieutenants were badly wounded and by 2.45 forty of her men were dead and ninety-six wounded. The rest fought like maniacs. Lieutenant Philip in his evidence at Williamson's court martial stated that: 'I am much afraid that a great part of our wounded will die, as they are in general dreadfully mangled. One of the men's wives assisted in firing a gun where her husband was quartered, though frequently requested to go below, but she would not be prevailed on to do so until a shot carried away one of her legs and wounded the other. As to the damage done to the ship, a description of it would fill sheets of paper. All our masts were so

Plan III

CAMPERDOWN
2.0 p.m.

TO TEXEL

VETERAN   Gelijkheid

ISIS   Beschermer

BELLIQUEUX

Hercules

TRIUMPH

LANCASTER

BEDFORD   Adm. de Vries

ARDENT   Vrijheid

   Staten-Generaal

VENERABLE

POWERFUL   Wassenaer
(struck 2.0)

CIRCE

DIRECTOR   Brutus

Leyden

Mars

Cerberus

RUSSELL   Jupiter (struck 1.45)

MONARCH

ADAMANT

Haarlem
(struck 1.15)

AGINCOURT

Alkmaar

MONTAGU

MONMOUTH   Monnikendam
(struck 2.0)

Delft   BEAULIEU

badly wounded that we could not set a sail on any of them and we were towed into port by the *Bedford*. It is indeed a wonder from the number of shot holes in her sides that we had not many more men killed. The first two broadsides of the Dutch were terrible; but after that, on an average, the British fired three guns to their one.'

The most realistic account of the hell which the cockpit became in a hard-fought action like this appears in the journal of the surgeon of the *Ardent*, Robert Young, who had no mate to assist him.

I was employed in operating and dressing till near 4.0 in the morning, the action beginning about 1.0 in the afternoon. So great was my fatigue that I began several amputations under a dread of sinking before I had secured the blood vessels.

Ninety wounded were brought down during the action. The whole cockpit deck, cabins, wing berths and part of the cable tier, together with my platform and preparations for dressing were covered with them. So that for a time they were laid on each other at the foot of the ladder where they were brought down, and I was obliged to go on deck to the Commanding Officer to state the situation and apply for men to go down the main hatchway and move the foremost of the wounded further forward into the tiers and wings, and thus make room in the cockpit. Numbers, about 16, mortally wounded, died after they were brought down, amongst whom was the brave and worthy Captain Burgess, whose corpse could with difficulty be conveyed to the starboard wing berth. Joseph Bonheur had his right thigh taken off by a cannon shot close to the pelvis, so that it was impossible to apply a tourniquet; his right arm was also shot to pieces. The stump of the thigh, which was very fleshy, presented a large and dreadful surface of mangled flesh. In this state he lived near two hours, perfectly sensible and incessantly calling out in a strong voice to me to assist him. The bleeding from the femoral artery, although so high up, must have been inconsiderable, and I observed it did not bleed as he lay. All the service I could render this unfortunate man was to put dressings over the part and give him drink. . . .

Melancholy cries for assistance were addressed to me from every side by wounded and dying, and piteous moans and bewailing from pain and despair. In the midst of these agonising scenes, I was able to preserve myself firm and collected, and embracing in my mind the whole of the situation, to direct my attention where the greatest and most essential services could be performed. Some with wounded, bad

indeed and painful, but slight in comparison with the dreadful condition of others, were most vociferous for my assistance. These I was
obliged to reprimand with severity, as their voices disturbed the last
moments of the dying. I cheered and commended the patient fortitude
of others, and sometimes extorted a smile of satisfaction from the
mangled sufferers, and succeeded to throw momentary gleams of
cheerfulness among so many horrors. The man whose leg I first
amputated had not uttered a groan from the time he was brought
down, and several, exulting in the news of the victory, declared they
regretted not the loss of their limbs.

An explosion of a salt box with several cartridges abreast of the
cockpit hatchway filled the hatchway with flame and in a moment
14 or 15 wretches tumbled down upon each other, their faces black
as a cinder, their clothes blown to shatters and their hats on fire. A
Corporal of Marines lived two hours after the action with all the
gluteal muscles shot away, so as to excavate the pelvis. Captain
Burgess' wound was of this nature, but he fortunately died almost
instantly.

After the action ceased, 15 or 16 dead bodies were removed before
it was possible to get a platform cleared and come at the materials for
operating and dressing, those I had prepared being covered over with
bodies and blood, and the store room door blocked up.

I have the satisfaction to say that of those who survived to undergo
amputation or be dressed, all were found the next morning in the
gunroom where they were placed in as comfortable a state as possible,
and on the third day were conveyed on shore in good spirits, cheering
the ship at going away, smoking their pipes and jesting as they sailed
along, and answering the cheers of the thousands of the populace
who received them on Yarmouth key.

Although no one had heard of the name of this obscure surgeon
until parts of his journal were printed in my *Medicine and the Navy* a
year or two ago, surely Robert Young deserves to be commemorated
among the naval heroes of that day. As for the men who bore their
wounds and underwent their amputations with such astonishing
fortitude (there was not even time enough to make them drunk or
to put a piece of leather between their jaws, as was usually done in
the days before anaesthetics), a Yarmouth merchant confirms Young's
description of the way in which they landed. He noted their 'haggard
and pale, though weather-beaten faces, which indicated heroically
suppressed pain. I shall not cease to remember the bearing of one

gallant fellow, on being accosted by a stranger who was induced to inveigh against the war. "Only a leg!" exclaimed Jack, endeavouring to lift himself upon his elbow. "Only a leg! Hurrah, Duncan for ever!"'

Before turning to the last scene on board the *Vrijheid*, we may describe the way Rear-Admiral Storij of the *States General* reached the Texel with what he calls eleven ships, though only seven vessels actually escaped from the battle. Storij succeeded De Winter in command of what was left of the fleet and it was he who was responsible for the abject surrender two years later. De Winter blamed him for deserting the flagship, but Storij claimed with justice that he had drawn the fire of the *Venerable* early in the battle. He then says that he attacked 'a ship of 84 guns', but no such ship existed: perhaps he meant the *Bedford* of 74. Indeed, few of the ships could recognise the identity of their opponents, particularly in the confusion which reigned around the two flagships. The usual entry in British logs is 'Engaged a yellow- or black-sided ship'.

Storij says that he continued fighting until three o'clock. 'While we were constantly repeating broadside after broadside, a fire broke out in our stern and between decks, but it was soon extinguished. All the ships were now so much disabled that they could no longer be managed and drove about in the greatest confusion. It was no longer possible to fire a single gun. . . . In a word, everything was carried away; we had shot in every part of the hull; and in this wretched state we floated about at the mercy of the waves. . . . The evening set in with heavy rain, which prevented us from seeing any of our ships but a few which had formed in the rear of the line. I then collected all the vessels belonging to my division that I could discover. At midnight I found that I had got together eleven sail. I endeavoured with them to collect the remainder of the squadron and stood towards the English fleet. At daybreak we saw them to windward of us at a short distance astern. We observed two ships making for the Texel. Upon coming near them we found they were English. They made sail, and we were not in a condition to chase them. I then continued to steer towards the Texel.'

To return to the battle itself. At about 2.30 the smoke lifted for a moment to enable De Winter, standing on the poop of the flagship, to see that all action had ceased in the rear. Since he was the only unwounded officer on the deck of the *Vrijheid*, he himself tried to hoist the signal for help, but in another burst of firing the halliards were shot out of his hand.

This firing came from the *Director*, Captain Bligh. Because she moved about more than any other ship, she saw more of what was going on, although it will be noted that Bligh was unaware of events in the van at the start of the action, since he belonged to Onslow's division, and hence he exaggerated the part by his ship in forcing the *Vrijheid* to surrender. (See Plan IV, p. 150.)

Though twelve years old, the *Director* was still noted for her good sailing qualities. She was only a fourth-rate of 64 guns and 491 men, but Bligh drove her into the thick of the fray in the Dutch rear without regard to the superior fire-power of his opponents, the *Alkmaar* and the *Haarlem*. When the latter struck, he left the *Adamant* to take possession of her and pushed up the Dutch line with the *Powerful* in company. There were so many ships locked in combat in the rear that he says 'it required great caution to prevent firing into one another'. In the centre, between the two dogfights at either end of the Dutch line, there was little going on, so he pressed on towards the beleaguered *Vrijheid*, apparently unaware that she had been engaged for some time by both the *Venerable* and the *Ardent*. This is how he describes the last hours of the battle:

> It appeared to me that some force was needed in the van, as we saw five ships unengaged and apparently not hurt and also the Dutch Commander-in-Chief without any ship of ours engaged with her. There was no time to be lost, as night was approaching, and as there were enough ships in our lee division about the rear of the enemy to take possession of them, I made sail (and passed the *Monarch*) engaging some of the centre ships, for I considered now the capture of the Dutch Commander-in-Chief's ship as likely to produce the capture of those ahead of him, and I desired my first lieutenant to inform the officers and men I was determined to be alongside the Dutch admiral.
>
> At 3.5 we began action with him, lying on his larboard quarter within twenty yards; by degrees we advanced alongside, firing tremendously at him, and then across his bows almost touching, when we carried away his fore mast, topmast, topgallant mast, and soon after his main mast, topmast and topgallant mast, together with his mizen mast, and left him nothing standing. The wreck lying all

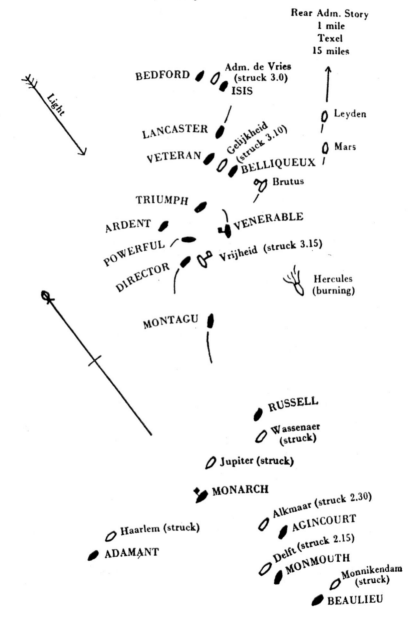

Plan IV
CAMPERDOWN
3.0 p.m.

over his starboard side, most of his guns were no use, I therefore hauled up along his starboard side and there we finished him, for at 3.55 he struck and the action ended.

Admiral Duncan, who we knew had severely engaged with the van of the enemy, had wore, and was now on the starboard tack standing from the shore about half a mile to leeward of the Dutch admiral. I therefore bore up to speak with him, when he hailed me to take possession of the *Vrijheid*, the ship we had just beaten, and I sent my first lieutenant on board in consequence. The Dutch admiral, Mr. De Winter, was taken on board of Admiral Duncan, and as the captain (Van Rossum) could not be removed owing to a death wound, my first lieutenant sent to me the captain-lieutenant, who was next in command.

As soon as the action ceased, my officers came to congratulate me and to say that there was not a man killed who they knew of, and of such good fortune I had no idea, for it passed belief.

There were only seven men wounded on board the *Director*, but on board the *Vrijheid* the carnage was terrible—fifty-eight killed and ninety-eight wounded. The Dutch claimed that she never surrendered because, though her colours were shot away again and again, they were always hoisted until there was no flag left to strike. At last an English officer hailed her through his speaking trumpet to find out if she had indeed surrendered. The reply was ambiguous: 'What do you think about it?'

Bligh's first lieutenant was called Richardson. He borrowed a jolly-boat from the *Circe* to row across to the stricken ship. He says that 'he found the admiral on his knees on the quarter-deck, holding a square sheet of lead which a carpenter was nailing over a shot hole in the bottom of a small punt about twelve feet in length, which was to have been launched for his escape. He surrendered, remarking "This my destiny was not foreseen", and taking leave of a young officer (I believe his nephew) who was desperately wounded, accompanied me to the gangway, the officers and crew making way for him, and many kneeling to take leave of their beloved commander.'

When De Winter came on board the *Venerable* he proffered his sword to Duncan. The latter refused it with the words: 'I would much rather take a brave man's hand than his sword.'

The incident is commemorated in the accompanying picture (26) by the artist Drummond who, in spite of his heroic-romantic style, brings out the comparative stature of the two admirals, as well as providing some interesting details, such as the net spread over the quarter-deck as protection against falling spars and yards, hence its name *sauve tête*. He has based his picture on a sketch sent by a Lieutenant Little to the painter Copley which is also reproduced (Fig. 25). On the back of the sketch Little writes: 'Enclosed I send you a view of the *Venerable*'s quarter-deck and poop, supposed to be standing near the mainmast and having it on your left hand. The cabin is cleared for action and the stern windows are seen. The number 1 shows the covering of the Hammacoes on the quarter-deck and poop [forming a breastwork for marines at action stations]. The number 2 shows the *sauve tête* netting. The number 3 shows part of the wheel. The rest needs no explanation.'

Duncan's despatch, together with a list of the ships of both fleets, is printed in the Appendix to this volume. It is dated the day after the battle and it pays deserved tribute to 'the most gallant manner' in which the enemy fought; but it does not mention the part played by Bligh. In view of the sentence that 'the carnage on board the two ships that bore the Admirals' flags has been beyond description', it was fitting that he ordered a thanksgiving service for the survivors before the ship turned for home.

In a private letter to Robert Dundas, Lord Advocate of Scotland, he gives some more details about his reception of De Winter:

> I feel perfectly satisfied. All was done that could be done. None have any fault to find. I have now in my possession three admirals Dutch, Admiral De Winter, Vice-Admiral Reuter, Rear-Admiral Meures. The admiral is on board with me, and a most agreeable man he is. He speaks English well and seems much pleased with his treatment. I have assured him, and with justice, that nothing could exceed his gallantry. He says nothing hurts him, but that he is the first Dutch admiral ever surrendered. So much more credit to me. He tells [me] the troops that embarked in the summer were 25,000 Dutch, destined for Ireland, but after August that expedition was given up. The government in Holland, much against his opinion, insisted on his going to sea, to show they had done so, and was just going to return, when I saw him. I believe the pilot and myself were the only two unhurt on the quarterdeck, and De Winter, who is as

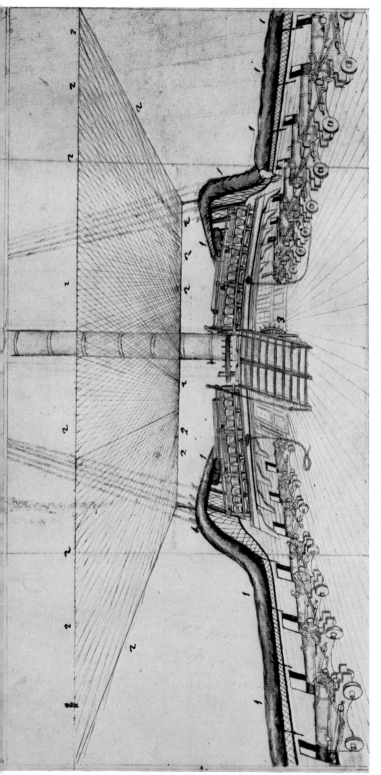

25 *Sketch of the quarterdeck of the 'Venerable' cleared for action*
     From a drawing in a letter by Lieut. John Little

26 (overleaf) *The surrender of Admiral de Winter on board the 'Venerable'*
     From an oil painting by S. Drummond

27 *The Battle of Camperdown*
From an oil painting by W. A. Knell

tall and big as I am, was the only one on his quarterdeck left alive. After all my fatigue, I am in perfect health and my usual spirits.

Duncan had already permitted the Dutch admiral to send a letter to his government, in which he blamed the centre ships for not closing the line when the enemy attacked 'with great resolution'. After paying tribute to his officers and men, De Winter concludes pathetically: 'Behold then the most unfortunate day of my life: every exertion that depends on manœuvre, or personal courage, was made by myself and many others on board, but in vain. Our enemies respect us on account of the obstinacy of our defence. No action could have been more bloody, for it was fatal for us. I shall have the honour of sending you a more accurate and minute account as soon as I find an opportunity. The condescension of the English admiral enables me to give you this previous notice. . . . I am, your unfortunate admiral, De Winter.'

But De Winter's second letter aroused violent criticism when it was printed in the English press. In this he attributed his defeat to the superior numbers of the British and to the refusal of Storij and others to obey his signals. He claimed that if they had done so, some English ships would have surrendered. An enraged English officer notes (in the Duncan MSS.) that it would have been better had he held his tongue 'than to have furnished the public with a garbled account which, for ought I know, might have been collected by people on shore who knew nothing of the action'. The contemporary historian James adds a more detailed rebuttal, but he concludes with a well deserved tribute: 'The shattered hulls and blood-besmeared decks of the prizes, and the almost equally damaged state of the principally engaged ships amongst those who had taken them, gave decided proofs that, although it had lain by so long, Batavian prowess still claimed the respect of an enemy and the applause of the world.'

9

The News of Victory

Dear Father,—I am come off safe and sound after having had a breeze with the Dutch. The battle lasted two hours when we killed one half and took the other half; so there is an end to Dutchmen. As to the particulars I can't tell you them just now, but when I get leave to go ashore and can come by a newspaper you shall have them all. For my part I minded nothing but my gun, except when we gave shouts of victory as the enemy's ships struck to us.

They say they are going to make a Lord of our Admiral. They can't make too much of him. He is a heart of oak; he is a seaman every inch of him, and as to a bit of a broadside, it only makes the old cock young again.

So wrote a young sailor when the ships returned to the Nore on October 17, while other units of the fleet made their way back to Yarmouth. It had been a difficult passage because of the damage suffered by ships on both sides. After an action with the French or Spanish fleet it was normal to see the rigging cut to pieces and many of the ships without masts or yards. But after Camperdown it was the hulls which were riddled with shot, because the Dutch adopted the English practice of close in-fighting and ship-destroying gunnery, whereas other navies preferred to fire on the up roll in order to damage the enemy's rigging, thus immobilising them. On October 12, 1797, the Dutch had no room to manœuvre, and the British, under Duncan's leadership, were determined not to let them get away, now that the two fleets had at last come to grips.

This applied more especially to the eleven prizes, of which James writes: 'As trophies, their appearance was gratifying; but as ships of war they were not the slightest acquisition to the navy of England.' The *Vrijheid*, totally dismasted, was towed across with difficulty by the *Montagu* and *Delft*. The *Delft* was taken in tow by the *Veteran*, but half-way across the latter's log notes: 'The people halloaing and making a great noise as if in distress. October 14. The prize still in tow. The people on board her showing a board with the words "The ship is sinking."' Such was the case. At half past three the *Delft* disappeared below the waves, after eighty-eight prisoners and a prize crew of sixty-nine had been taken off. Two of the captured frigates were wrecked on the Dutch coast because they were so badly damaged that they were unmanageable.

None of this affected the national outburst of elation which greeted Duncan on his arrival at the Nore. Eleven prizes out of eighteen ships engaged was a remarkable record, over twice the number taken at the battle of St. Vincent and only surpassed by Nelson's achievement the following year at the Nile.

On October 18 the *Courier* announced the arrival of the ships at Yarmouth. Special mention was made of Duncan's indebtedness to Clerk of Eldin, though his name was spelled wrong. 'It is supposed that Admiral Duncan will net about £60,000 prize money.' This was a journalist's guess, because it was years before the Prize Courts adjudicated the final amount due for distribution. From Duncan's own prize accounts we know that in January 1798 his brokers informed him that £150,000 was the sum to be divided and that they had bought stock for him at one-eighth below the market price because the Stock Exchange 'applauded him' (surely a unique occurrence in history). On May 9 he was paid a first dividend of £10,000, but claims and counter-claims continued for the next two years, so that it is impossible to assess the final amount. One of the most intransigent claimants was Captain Bligh, who continued to exaggerate his share in the capture of the *Vrijheid*. After every naval victory in those days there was much unsavoury litigation, even between such men as St. Vincent and Nelson.

Honours fell thick and fast upon the victorious admiral. On the day he landed he was created Baron Duncan of Lundie (the family estate in Scotland) and Viscount Duncan of Camperdown. Onslow was created a baronet. Trollope and Fairfax, the bearer of despatches, were knighted. As after St. Vincent, gold medals were awarded to all the admirals and captains. Duncan was given the Freedom of the City of London and presented with a sword worth 200 guineas.

Lloyd's promptly opened a Patriotic Fund for the benefit of the 812 wounded and the relations of the 228 killed. Other sources give the figures of 622 wounded and 203 killed, and the Dutch equivalents as 540 killed, 620 wounded, with 3775 prisoners, the highest in any battle save Trafalgar. The Lloyd's Fund collected from all part of the kingdom, amounted to £52,609 10s. 10d., a handsome sum in those days.

We can follow the celebrations in the popular press. On October 19 it was announced that both the Theatre Royal, Covent Garden and the Theatre Royal, Drury Lane, would conclude their performances with representations of the Dutch fleet striking their colours to the tune of *Rule Britannia*. On October 23 there was a general thanksgiving at St. Paul's Cathedral and a Grand Dinner given by the Secretary of the Admiralty. On November 4 Spencer moved a vote of thanks in the House of Lords, which was seconded by Admiral Hood and the Duke of Clarence, the future William IV and the last Lord High Admiral of England. Duncan, always a man of few words, actually began his reply with the words, 'Not accustomed to speak in public. . . .'

On his arrival in London he went to the lodgings of his brother-in-law in Lincoln's Inn Fields to take him out to dinner. They went to a coffee house in Covent Garden, where they had scarcely sat down before a note was sent to William Dundas asking if his tall friend was not Admiral Duncan. When this was admitted, someone jumped on a table to ask all those present to drink his health. 'The uproar was tremendous. The admiral got on his legs and in a stentorian voice said, "Gentlemen, I thank you!" Not another word. They all cheered louder than ever, and Sheridan, who was having some quieter orgies of his own in a private room upstairs, sent to ascertain what the tumult was about. They began vociferating in their turn and my Uncle and the admiral got to a hackney coach at the door to escape. The people outside heard who they were, took the horses out of the coach and drew it round Covent Garden, and it was with difficulty they were allowed to go home.' The same thing happened on November 10 when, on his way to receive the Freedom of the City, the crowd detached the horses from his carriage on Ludgate Hill and drew it in triumph to Guildhall.

There was only one flaw in the general enthusiasm. On December

4 a court martial assembled at Sheerness to try John Williamson, captain of the *Agincourt*. It is something of a mystery how Williamson ever reached the rank of captain. As a lieutenant on Cook's last voyage (on which Bligh, now a witness, also sailed) he had disgraced himself by an act of cowardice which was partly responsible for Cook's death. Williamson was in charge of the boats which landed Cook at Hawaii. When the mob of natives attacked the captain, the latter retreated towards the beach shouting to the boats to pull closer in. According to his own account, Williamson mistook the signal and pulled farther out, although another boat obeyed. Four minutes later Cook was stabbed in the back and some of the marines were wounded as they dashed into the sea. Still Williamson did nothing; nor did he even attempt to recover the captain's body when the riot died down. On the voyage home the captain of marines challenged him to a duel, but Williamson refused to fight. Now, sixteen years later, he met the end of his professional career.

The burden of the voluminous evidence was that everyone was so busy fighting that they never noticed where Williamson was: it was only afterwards that the absence of his ship from her proper station was remarked on. The court summarised the charges against him and its findings in these words:

> That the said John Williamson did not upon that day, upon signal and order of fight and upon sight of several of the enemy's ships which it was his duty to engage, do his duty, and obey such signals, and also for that he did, on the said eleventh day of October last during the time of action, through cowardice, negligence or disaffection keep back and did not come into the fight or engagement, and did not do his utmost to take or destroy such of the enemy's ships as it was his duty to engage, and to assist and relieve such of His Majesty's ships as it was his duty to assist and relieve; and having heard the witnesses produced in support of the charges, and having heard what he had to allege in his defence, and having maturely and deliberately weighed and considered the whole: the Court is of opinion that the charges of cowardice and disaffection have not been proved, that the other parts of the charge have been proved in part. Therefore, in consideration of the case and the nature and degree of the offence, the Court doth adjudge the said Captain John Williamson to be placed at the bottom of the captain's list and rendered incapable of ever serving on board

any of His Majesty's ships or vessels in the Royal Navy, and he is hereby sentenced accordingly.

To turn to a more pleasant aspect of the aftermath of victory. The treatment of De Winter as a prisoner could not have been more honourable. The English have always respected a doughty fighter. From the moment of his surrender he was treated with the utmost consideration. The Secretary of the Admiralty invited him to a private dinner party, and with Duncan De Winter struck up a lifelong friendship which is expressed in the many letters, usually in French, which he subsequently wrote to him. This is the conclusion of one such letter, written three months after his capture: 'Accept, my Lord, my eternal respect and friendship; at your leisure hour sometimes bestow a thought upon a man whom you have for ever obliged, and who will never cease to be with the highest esteem, and with the most sincere attachment, your most obedient and most humble servant. DE WINTER.'

When Duncan arranged for his repatriation, along with Rear-Admiral Meures, because of the news that his wife had suffered a stroke, De Winter's gratitude knew no bounds. He gave his parole never to fight the English again, which meant that on his return to Holland he left the sea for diplomacy. However, after the Peace of Amiens (and after Napoleon had abolished the ancient and civilised customs of parole and exchange) he returned to the sea in command of an expedition against the Barbary corsairs. He was among the earliest recipients of the Legion of Honour and he remained in nominal command of the Dutch navy until 1811. He died in Paris the next year and was buried in the Pantheon with all the panoply of a leading figure of the Empire.

Both the British heroes of this book lived to a ripe old age: St. Vincent to the age of eighty-nine and Duncan to that of seventy-three. After Camperdown Duncan continued in command of the North Sea fleet until 1800, when he retired to his family estate in Scotland, where the figurehead of the *Vrijheid* was installed in the grounds of Lundie House. He offered his services on the renewal of war, but they were declined in view of his advanced age. He died in 1804, within a week of the loss of his old flagship, the *Venerable*, which was wrecked on Berry Head in a storm. It was a miracle she had lasted so long.

One of the reasons why the news of the victory of Camperdown was received so enthusiastically was because it wiped away the stain on the honour of the Royal Navy left by the mutinies. With the two victories described in this book, Britain entered the Nelsonian period, when a further series of victories founded that supremacy at sea which remained unchallenged until the beginning of the twentieth century. Those victories won for the Navy a renewed popularity which had been dimmed by its failures and dissensions during the War of American Independence. It cannot be pretended that the naval service was ever popular among those who were liable to impressment; but with the country as a whole it now enjoyed a degree of admiration which the Army never achieved until the end of the Peninsular War. With the battles of St. Vincent and Camperdown a new and blatant patriotism was born, which enabled this country to survive the long years of war that lay ahead. This patriotism was centred on the achievements of 'our gallant tars', as they were unashamedly called, and it culminated in the apotheosis of Nelson.

Such was the mood expressed in a song which was widely sung in the winter months after Duncan's victory at Camperdown:

> *St. Vincent drubbed the Dons, Earl Howe he drubbed Monsieur,*
> *And gallant Duncan now has soundly drubbed Mynheer;*
> *The Spanish, French and Dutch, tho' all united be,*
> *Fear not, Britannia cries, My Tars can beat all three.*

> Chorus
> *Monsieurs, Mynheers and Dons, your Country's empty boast,*
> *Our Tars can beat all three, each on his native coast.*

Appendix 1

THE ST. VINCENT DESPATCH

To the Secretary of the Admiralty

Victory
Lagos Bay
February 16, 1797

Sir,—The hopes of falling in with the Spanish fleet, expressed in my letter to you of the 13th instant, were confirmed last night, by our distinctly hearing the report of their signal guns, and by intelligence received from Captain Foote of H.M. ship the *Niger*, who had, with equal judgement and perseverance kept company with them for several days, on my prescribed rendezvous, which from the strong south-east winds I have never been able to reach, and that they were not more than the distance of three or four leagues from us. I anxiously awaited the dawn of the day, when, being on the starboard tack, Cape St. Vincent bearing east by north eight leagues, I had the satisfaction of seeing a number of ships extending from south-west to south, the wind then at west by south. At 49 minutes past ten, the weather being extremely hazy, *La Bonne Citoyenne* made the signal that the ships seen were of the line, 27 in number. His Majesty's squadron under my command, consisting of 15 ships of the line, named in the margin, happily formed in the most compact order of sailing, in two lines. By carrying a press of sail, I was fortunate in getting with the enemy's fleet at half-past eleven o'clock before it had time to connect and form a regular order of battle. Such a moment was not to be lost; and, confident in the skill, valour and discipline of the officers and men I had the happiness to command, and judging that the honour of His Majesty's arms, and the circumstances of war in these seas, required a considerable degree of enterprise, I felt myself justified in departing from the regular system; and, passing through their fleet, in a line formed with the utmost celerity, tacked, and thereby separated one-third from the main body; after a partial cannonade, which prevented their re-junction until evening, and, by the very great exertions of the ships which had the good fortune to arrive up with the enemy on the larboard tack, the ships named in the margin were captured, and the action ceased about five o'clock in the evening.

I enclose the most correct list I have been able to obtain of the Spanish fleet opposed to me, amounting to 27 sail of the line, and an account of the killed and wounded in H.M. ships, as well as those taken from the enemy. The moment the latter (almost totally dis-masted) and H.M. ships the *Captain* and the *Culloden* are in a state to put to sea, I shall avail myself of the first favourable wind to proceed off Cape St. Vincent, on my way to Lisbon.

Captain Calder, whose able assistance has greatly contributed to the public service during my command, is the bearer of this, and will particularly describe to the Lords Commissioners of the Admiralty the movements of the squadron on the 14th, and the present state of it.

I am, Sir, Etc.,

J. JERVIS.

LIST OF BRITISH SHIPS AT THE BATTLE
OF ST. VINCENT

FEBRUARY 14, 1797

Ship	Guns	Commander
Victory	100	Admiral Sir John Jervis
		Captain R. Calder
Captain	74	Commodore H. Nelson
		Captain R. W. Miller
Blenheim	90	T. L. Frederick
Culloden	74	T. Troubridge
Excellent	74	C. Collingwood
Irresistible	74	G. Martin
Prince George	98	Rear-Admiral Parker
		Captain V. T. Irwin
Orion	74	Sir J. Saumarez
Goliath	74	Sir C. H. Knowles
Namur	90	J. H. Whitshed
Barfleur	98	Vice-Admiral Waldegrave
		Captain J. R. Dacres
Colossus	74	G. Murray
Diadem	64	G. H. Towry
Egmont	74	J. Sutton
Britannia	100	Vice-Admiral Thompson
		Captain T. Foley

FRIGATES, ETC.

Lively	32	Lord Garlies
La Minerve	38	G. Cockburn
Niger	32	E. J. Foote
Southampton	32	J. McNamara
La Bonne Citoyenne	18	C. Lindsay
Raven brig	18	W. Prowse
Fox cutter	12	Lt. Gibson

LIST OF SPANISH SHIPS AT THE BATTLE
OF ST. VINCENT

FEBRUARY 14, 1797

Ship	Guns	Commander
Atlante	74	G. Vallego
Bahama	74	Admiral D. de Nava
Pelayo	74	C. Valdes
San Pablo	74	B. de Cisneros
Neptuno	84	J. L. Goicoechea
Concepcion	112	Admiral Morales de los Rios
San Domingo	74	M. de Torres
Conquistadore	74	J. Butler
San Juan Nepomuceno	74	A. Boneo
San Genaro	74	A. Villavicencio
Mexicano	112	Admiral P. de Cardenas
Terrible	74	F. Uriarte
Oriente	74	J. Suarez
Soberano	74	J. V. Yanez
Santissimo Trinidada	136	Admiral J. de Cordova
*San Nicolas	84	T. Geraldino
*San Ysidro	74	D. T. Argumosa
*Salvador del Mundo	112	D. A. Yepes
*San Josef	112	Admiral F. J. Winthuysen
San Ildefonso	74	R. Maestre
Conde de Regla	112	Admiral P. de Cardenas
San Firmin	74	J. de Torres
Principe de Asturias	112	Admiral J. J. Moreno
San Antonio	74	S. Medina
San Francisco de Paulo	74	J. de Guimbarda
Firme	74	B. Ayala
Glorioso	74	J. Aguizze

* Signifies captured ships.

APPENDIX I

FRIGATES AND URCAS

Ship	Guns	Ship	Guns
Brigida	34	Asuncion (urca)	28
Perla	34	San Justa (urca)	18
Mercedes	34	San Balbino (urca)	20
Vigilante brig	12	San Paulo (urca)	20
Matilda	34		
Diana	34		
Atocha	34		
Ceres	34		

Appendix 11

THE CAMPERDOWN DESPATCH

To the Secretary of the Admiralty

Venerable, at sea:
October 13, 1797,
off the coast of Holland

SIR,—Be pleased to acquaint the Lords Commissioners of the
Admiralty, that, judging it of Consequence their Lordships should
have as early Information as possible of the Defeat of the Dutch
fleet under the command of Admiral De Winter, I despatched the
Rose cutter at three p.m. on the 12th instant, with a short Letter to
you, immediately after the Action was ended. I have now to acquaint
you, for their Lordships' Information, that on the Night of the
10th [11th] instant, after I had sent away my Letter to you, of that
Date, I placed my Squadron in such Situation as to prevent the
Enemy from returning to the Texel without my falling in with them.
At nine o'clock in on the Morning of the 11th [12th] I got Sight of
Captain Trollope's Squadron, with Signals flying for an Enemy to
Leeward; I immediately gave Chase, and soon got Sight of them,
forming Line on the Larboard Tack to receive us, the wind at NW.
As we approached near I made the Signal for the Squadron to
shorten sail, in order to connect them; soon after I saw land between
Camperdown and Egmont, about nine Miles to Leeward of the
Enemy, and finding there was no Time to be lost in making the
Attack, I made the Signal to bear up, break the Enemy's Line, and
engage them to Leeward, each Ship her Opponent, by which I got
between them and the Land, whither they were fast approaching.
My Signals were obeyed with great Promptitude and Vice-Admiral
Onslow, in the *Monarch,* bore down on the Enemy's Rear in the
most gallant manner, his Division following his Example; and the
Action commenced about Forty Minutes past Twelve o'clock. The
Venerable soon got through the Enemy's Line, and I began a close

Action, with my Division on their Van, which lasted near Two Hours and a Half, when I observed all the Masts of the Dutch Admiral's Ship to go by the Board; she was however, defended for some Time in a most gallant Manner; but being overpressed by Numbers, her Colours were struck, and Admiral De Winter was soon brought on Board the *Venerable*. On looking round me I observed the Ship bearing the Vice-Admiral's Flag was also dismasted, and had surrendered to Vice-Admiral Onslow; and that many others had likewise struck. Finding that we were in Nine Fathoms Water, and not farther than Five Miles from the Land, my Attention was so much taken up in getting the Heads of the disabled Ships off Shore, that I was not able to distinguish the Number of Ships captured; and the Wind having been constant on the Land since, we have unavoidably been much dispersed, so that I have not been able to gain an exact Account of them, but we have taken Possession of Eight or Nine; more of them had struck, but taking Advantage of the Night, and being so near their own Coast, they succeeded in getting off, and some of them were seen going into the Texel the next Morning.

It is with the greatest Pleasure and Satisfaction I make known to their Lordships the very gallant Behaviour of Vice-Admiral Onslow, the Captains, Officers, Seamen and Marines of the Squadron, who all appeared actuated with the truly British Spirit, at least those that I had an Opportunity of seeing.

One of the Enemy's Ships caught Fire in the Action and drove very near the *Venerable*; but I have the Pleasure to say it was extinguished, and she is one of the Ships in our Possession. The Squadron has suffered much in their Masts, Yards and Rigging, and many of them have lost a Number of Men; however, in no Proportion to that of the Enemy. The Carnage on Board the Two Ships that bore the Admiral's Flags has been beyond all Description; thay have no less than 250 Men killed or wounded on Board of each Ship; and here I have to lament the Loss of Captain Burgess of H.M. Ship the *Ardent*, who brought that Ship into Action in the most gallant and masterly Manner, but was unfortunately killed soon after. However, the Ship continued the Action until quite disabled. The Public lost a good and gallant Officer in Captain Burgess, and I, with others, a sincere Friend.

Captain Trollope's Exertions and active good Conduct in keeping Sight of the Enemy's Fleet until I came up, have been truly meritorious, and, I trust, will meet a just Reward.

I send this by Captain Fairfax, by whose able Advice I profited much during the Action, and who will give their Lordships any further Particulars they may wish to know.

As most of the Ships of the Squadron are much disabled, and several of the Prizes dismasted, I shall make the best of my Way to the Nore.

I herewith transmit you a List of Killed and Wounded on Board such of the Squadron as I have been able to collect; a List of the Enemy's Fleet opposed to my Squadron, and my Line of Battle on the Day of Action.

I am, Sir, Your most obedient humble Servant,
ADAM DUNCAN.

THE BRITISH AND DUTCH FLEETS AT CAMPERDOWN

(The Dutch ships are printed in the order opposite those which they engaged)

British	Dutch
Isis, 50, Capt. W. Mitchell	**Gelijkheid*, 68, Capt. Ruyse
Lancaster, 64, Capt. J. Wells	*Beschermer*, 56, Capt. Hinxtt
Belliqueux, 64, Capt. J. Inglis	**Hercules*, 64, Capt. Rysoort
Bedford, 74, Capt. Sir T. Byard	**De Vries*, 68, Capt. J. B. Zegers
Ardent, 64, Capt. R. Burgess	**Vrijheid*, 74, Adm. de Winter
Venerable, 74, Adm. Duncan	*States General*, 74, Adm. Storij
Triumph, 74, Capt. W. H. Essington	**Wassenaer*, 64, Capt. Holland
Veteran, 64, Capt. G. Gregory	*Cerberus*, 68, Capt. Jacobson
Monarch, 74, Vice-Adm. R. Onslow	**Jupiter*, 74, Adm. Reyntjes
Powerful, 74, Capt. W. O'Bryen Drury	**Haarlem*, 68, Capt. Wiggerts
Director, 64, Capt. W. Bligh	**Alkmaar*, 56, Capt. Kraft
Russell, 74, Capt. H. Trollope	**Delft*, 56, Capt. Verdoorn
Monmouth, 64, Capt. J. Walker	**Monnikendam*, 44, Capt. Lancaster
Montagu, 74, Capt. J. Knight	**Embuscade*, 32, Capt. Huys
Adamant, 50, Capt. W. Hotham	*Batavier*, 56, Capt. Souters
Agincourt, 64, Capt. J. Williamson	*Brutus*, 74, Adm. Bloys
	Leyden, 68, Capt. Musquetier
	Mars, 44, Capt. Kolff

Frigates etc.	*Frigates etc.*
Beaulieu	*Waaksaamheid*
Rose	*Minerva*
King George	*Galatea*
Active	*Atalanta*
Diligent	*Heldin*
Speculator	*Daphne*
Circe	*Ajax*
Martin	

* Signifies captured ships.

Sources

GENERAL AND MANUSCRIPTS

Logs of the Great Sea Fights, ed. Sturges Jackson. Navy Records Society (1899).
The Spencer Papers, ed. J. S. Corbett. Navy Records Society (1894). Vols. 1, 2.
A Naval History of Great Britain, W. James (1837).
Projets et Tentatives de Débarquement aux Iles Britanniques, Desbrière. Vol. I (1900).
The St. Vincent Papers are at the British Museum (Add. MSS. 31,159).
The Duncan Papers are at the National Maritime Museum.

BANTRY BAY

E. H. Stuart Jones, *An Invasion that Failed* (1950).
F. MacDermot, *Wolfe Tone* (1939).
The Keith Papers, Vol. II, ed. C. Lloyd, Navy Records Society (1947).
C. Northcote Parkinson, *Edward Pellew, Lord Exmouth* (1934).

ST VINCENT AND THE MEDITERRANEAN FLEET

J. S. Tucker, *Lief of Lord St. Vincent* (1844).
E. P. Brenton, *Life of Lord St. Vincent* (1838).
Sir John Ross, *Life of De Saumarez* (1838).
J. Drinkwater-Bethune, *Narrative of the Proceedings of the British Fleet . . .* (1797, 1840).
C. F. Duro, *Armada Espanola*, Vol. VIII (1902).
A. H. Taylor, 'Note on the Battle of St. Vincent', *Mariner's Mirror* (1954).
Private Correspondence of Admiral Lord Collingwood, ed. E. Hughes, Navy Records Society (1957).
Nelson's Letters to his Wife, ed. G. P. Naish. Navy Records Society (1958).
L. Kennedy, *Nelson's Band of Brothers* (1951).

THE MUTINIES

C. Gill, *The Naval Mutinies of 1797* (1913).
G. Manwaring and B. Dobrée, *The Floating Republic* (1935).
C. Lloyd, 'New Light on the Mutiny at the Nore', *Mariner's Mirror* (1960).

CAMPERDOWN

Earl of Camperdown, *Admiral Duncan* (1898).
A. H. Taylor, 'William Bligh at Camperdown', *Mariner's Mirror* (1937).
C. Lloyd and J. L. S. Coulter, *Medicine and the Navy*, Vol. III (1961).

INDEX

Index

The numerals in **heavy type** refer to the *figure numbers* of the illustrations